Manpower and the Growth of
PRODUCER SERVICES

Manpower and the Growth of
PRODUCER
SERVICES

by HARRY I. GREENFIELD

FOREWORD BY ELI GINZBERG

Columbia University Press

NEW YORK & LONDON 1966

The material in this project was prepared under a contract from the Office of Manpower Policy, Evaluation and Research, U.S. Department of Labor, under the authority of Title 1 of the Manpower Development and Training Act of 1962, as amended. Researchers undertaking such projects under Government sponsorship are encouraged to express freely their professional judgment. Therefore, points of view or opinions stated in this document do not necessarily represent the official position or policy of the Department of Labor.

To my Wife and Children

FOREWORD

Two out of every three American workers are employed today in the services sector of the economy. Only one in three still earns his livelihood in agriculture, mining, manufacturing, or construction, which together comprise the goods-producing sector. Moreover, the services sector, which provides employment for the majority of the population, has been growing rapidly in the last few decades.

Despite the growing significance of the services sector, it has been subjected only infrequently to detailed study. Professor George Stigler broke important ground with his investigations of the services industries in 1956; and Dr. Victor Fuchs is currently engaged in a large-scale inquiry into the productivity of the services sector. Both of these efforts as well as several related undertakings—those of Fabricant, Barger, Hultgren and Goldsmith are particularly important—have been carried out under the auspices of the National Bureau of Economic Research.

A word about the origin of the present monograph. Under a contract from the Office of Manpower Policy, Evaluation, and Research of the United States Department of Labor, the Conservation of Human Resources Project of Columbia University has been engaged during the past several years in a series of studies under the rubric, "Manpower Resources and Economic Growth." Professor Dale L. Hiestand has served as Project Director of these studies. In the first product of this research investigation, *The Pluralistic Economy*, we submitted our conclusion that the services sector had played a prominent part in the expansion of the American economy since 1940 and that it loomed particularly important in the rapid growth of the not-for-profit sector—that is, in government and nonprofit institutions.

The original plan of research provided for an investigation of the not-for-profit sector as well as for several case studies which we hoped would illuminate the dynamics of employment expansion in selected segments of the economy. To this end an inquiry was undertaken by Professor James W. Kuhn into *Scientific and Managerial Manpower in Nuclear Industry,* the specific aim of which was to assess the role of highly skilled manpower in the diffusion of nuclear technology.

The present volume presents the results of the second case study, which was structured to enable us to explore in depth the growth of services in the private sector of the economy.

As I have noted, we had been struck by the fact that several of the fastest growing service fields, such as health and education, were in the not-for-profit sector. But the continuing importance of the private sector for the nation's economic progress led us to explore the expansion of services in that sector. We therefore singled out "business services" for analysis. They had attracted much less attention than consumer services, and they were by definition more likely to be anchored in profit-seeking enterprises.

That was our assumption, but we early recognized that while this assumption was generally valid, we had to make allowance for the fact that the production and sale of many business services were connected with the not-for-profit sector as well—that is, these services were either produced by government or nonprofit institutions or they were sold to them. It appeared, therefore, that the term "business services" was something of a misnomer. We consequently substituted the term "producer services" to indicate that these are services which are important to different types of enterprises—profit, nonprofit, and governmental—all of which are engaged in the further production of goods and services.

It was our good fortune at the outset of this investigation to have ready access to several enterprises engaged in producer services, including one of the largest and most diversified organizations in the maintenance field whose business spans the whole of the United States and includes such functions as building maintenance, the servicing of planes, and the disposal of atomic waste. The cooperation of the managements of these several organizations was a strategic factor in the successful completion of our investigation.

As we began to explore the many dimensions of producer services, Professor Harry Greenfield, the principal investigator, found it helpful to make adaptations in the long-established concepts of time, durability, and investment. On the basis of his carry-over of concepts which have long proved constructive in the analysis of commodities, he was able to construct a systematic and coherent classification scheme for services. For the first time, we have a scheme which enables us to differentiate services in terms of degree of their perishability or durability; and to distinguish decision-making in services (according to whether they support current output or have the quality of a long-term investment). There is much in Professor Greenfield's suggestive conceptual framework that the interested reader will want to probe and ponder.

The structure of this monograph is based on the underlying orientation of our research, which is to study the interrelations between the growth of an industry and the growth of employment associated with it. Because of our central concern with manpower we have sought to learn as much as possible in this exploratory undertaking about the ways in which the availability of persons and skills has facilitated the growth of producer services and, in turn, about the ways in which the demand for producer services has had important consequences for the expansion of employment.

We did, however, encounter serious difficulties in undertaking and carrying out this inquiry into the dynamics of producer services, because of the limitations of the data available and because of an imperfect fit between the new concepts and these data. We overcame these difficulties partly through improvisation and partly by accepting findings that were clearly no better than first approximations.

Despite these limitations, Professor Greenfield sets forth in systematic fashion a considerable amount of information about producer services as a whole as well as about the newer, dynamic producer services which have not been analyzed in depth. Dr. Greenfield provides detailed data about the characteristics of the manpower used by the different fields within the service sector; regional patterns reflecting the present concentration and differential growth of producer services in the recent past; and the interrelations between the expansion of the industries they service and their own expansion.

Among the more important findings that emerge from these and his other analyses are the following. First, the accepted prototype of the service sector as a field which employs a large number of unskilled persons at low wages does not fit the reality of many producer services, which make substantial use of professional and trained personnel and where employees (and self-employed owners) earn more than the national average. Second, the location of producer services appears to be determined in considerable measure by the location of industrial plants and by the density of urban concentration. Third, there are strong links between the expansion of one particular producer service and the expansion of others, since so many producer services firms are themselves dependent on the purchase of external services. Fourth, the regional growth of producer services, at least in the 1950–1960 decade, appeared to be closely related to the growth of population, total economic growth, and the expansion of government operations.

Dr. Greenfield found that producer services account for approximately a quarter of the national income and a sixth of total employment. Moreover, between 1950 and 1960, characteristic producer services grew more rapidly than did the economy as a whole. Clearly, here is a segment of the services sector that deserves more attention from economists. But if research is to be productive, more and better data must be collected and organized. We hope that those in the best position to improve the quality and quantity of data collection, particularly the agencies of the federal government, will recognize the opportunities and respond to them.

The bearing of this monograph on manpower policy is obvious: First and most important is the potential within producer services for the generation of employment, including the employment of individuals with widely different backgrounds. Second, the availability of producer services, adequate in scope and quality, appears to be an important determinant of the rate of economic and employment expansion in other sectors. Therefore, public policy should consider the potentialities of stimulating both economic expansion and particularly job expansion through actions aimed at strengthening selected producer services. Finally, the fact that enterprises which furnish many producer services can start and grow with very small capitalization, and in the process of expansion can contribute directly and indirectly to the creation of new jobs, underscores the importance of various types of action, private, nonprofit and government, which are aimed at stimulating the generation and expansion of such enterprises. For new and expanding industries are the *sine qua non* for the growth of employment.

ELI GINZBERG
Director
Conservation of
* Human Resources Project*
Columbia University

July, 1966

ACKNOWLEDGMENTS

This monograph owes so much to the staff of the Conservation of Human Resources Project of Columbia University that it is often difficult for me to determine where my thoughts left off and those of the staff began—and vice versa. I am indebted, in the first instance, to Professor Eli Ginzberg not only for providing me with the opportunity to undertake this study but also for his constructive and sympathetic guidance throughout. Professor Dale L. Hiestand likewise helped to guide me through the many conceptual and statistical labyrinths I encountered from the first draft of the manuscript through to the last. Dr. Beatrice Reubens aided in the clarification of my early thoughts and also contributed to the material in Chapter V.

Mr. Richard V. Knight worked up most of the regional data of Chapter VI and provided many valuable analytic insights as well. Mrs. Roberta Handwerger responded cheerfully to my requests for research assistance.

I should like especially to acknowledge the constructive and highly knowledgeable critique which the monograph received at the hands of Dr. Victor R. Fuchs of the National Bureau of Economic Research.

Thanks are also due to the many research workers both in government departments and in private firms and research agencies who were extremely cooperative in providing the information I requested.

For excellent clerical and typing assistance during the several drafts of the manuscript I am deeply grateful to Mrs. Sylvia Leef, Miss Paula Frank, and Miss Carol Fortin. Mrs. Ruth Szold Ginzberg's editorial skill greatly improved the readability of the manuscript. The invaluable assistance of Mrs. Marian Maury of the Columbia University Press in preparing the manuscript for publication is gratefully acknowledged.

All of the conceptual lapses and factual errors in this monograph were produced under conditions of complete monopoly.

HARRY I. GREENFIELD

Columbia University
July, 1966

see Contracting costs

CONTENTS

Chapter I

WHAT ARE PRODUCER SERVICES?

There is widespread recognition that we are experiencing a revolutionary change in the structure of the American economy. Today only one out of every three workers is employed in the production of goods; all other workers have jobs in what is defined as the services sector. As one writer put it recently:

This country is pioneering in a new stage of economic development. We are now a "service economy" that is, we are the first nation in the history of the world in which more than half of the employed population is not involved in the production of food, clothing, houses, automobiles and other tangible goods.[1]

The size and significance of the services sector notwithstanding, it has only occasionally been studied in depth, and then primarily with attention to "consumer services." Another important segment of the services sector, namely "producer services," which is functionally quite distinct from the former, has been almost entirely overlooked.

This monograph is focused specifically on "producer services," that is, those services which business firms, nonprofit institutions, and governments provide and usually sell to the producer rather than to the consumer. This involves a very wide range of activities from firms that specialize in data processing to those that repair blast furnaces; from firms that specialize in the maintenance of office buildings to those that rent equipment to hotels.

[1] Victor R. Fuchs, "The Growing Importance of the Service Industries," *The Journal of Business of the University of Chicago*, XXXVIII (October, 1965), 344.

There are two basic reasons for focusing on producer services. Both have already been suggested but they should be made explicit. The growth of the services sector of the economy has been very rapid, and presumably this will be found to be the case with respect to the producer services segment. Since the continuing growth of the economy depends not only on the experience of established industries but also and very importantly on the creation of new ones, a study in depth of producer services should contribute new insights into and understanding of the processes of growth.

But in addition to this consideration, the broad service sector is now the principal area for job creation and expansion. Hence, in an economy such as ours, where public concern with the growth of employment opportunities has taken precedence even over the growth of income, it is desirable to study the manpower parameters of the services field in general and of producer services in particular. What has been the rate of growth in employment in producer services and what are the prospects for future growth? What kinds of people and skills are used by firms and industries producing such services? And there are other manpower dimensions dealing with training, mobility, and wages that should likewise be appraised.

The major emphasis of the present monograph is on the factors affecting the supply of and demand for producer services, that is to say, services (not material goods) that enterprises obtain from one another. In a pluralistic economy, firms not only purchase services from other firms but, in addition, either purchase or obtain "free" services from all levels of government, as well as from nonprofit organizations such as trade associations. Our attention in the present work will be primarily with the market relationships in the services, that is, on the direct purchase of services by one business firm from another. While we are cognizant of the fact that "service" or "nonproduction" occupations and functions have also grown in importance within the firm itself, our primary concern is with the nature of the external enterprises from which firms purchase all types of services.

Since relatively little prior work has focused on producer services, our first and overriding task will be to extend the conceptual framework and to deepen the statistical underpinnings necessary for gaining more understanding of the dynamics of this segment of our economy. But in pursuing this task we will remain particularly alert to manpower considerations, since this monograph grows out of our continuing concern with the interrelations between manpower resources and economic growth.

Goods and Services: Some Basic Distinctions

Since current definitions of "services" stem partly from the usage of that term by economists, it may be instructive at this point to trace briefly the changes in that concept in economic literature in order to place the definitions offered here in perspective.

Early discussions of the nature of economic goods and wealth were heavily influenced by the physiocratic approach, which defined national income and wealth as an aggregate only of consumable commodities. Paul Studenski has remarked that, "as to the nonagricultural occupations, the Physiocrats took the position that although they were not necessarily useless they were sterile in the sense that they did no more than return their costs." [2]

Adam Smith criticized the physiocrats for classifying manufacturing, trade, and transportation as sterile occupations, insisting that these branches of "material goods production" were just as capable of returning a net income to the producers as was agriculture, this net income taking the form of profits in-

[2] Paul Studenski, *The Income of Nations*, p. 15.

stead of net rent.[3] However, Smith made a distinction between "productive" and "unproductive" labor. In his words, "the labor of a manufacturer adds generally to the value of the materials which he works upon. . . . The labor of a menial servant, on the contrary, adds to the value of nothing." [4] The reason for this view, according to Smith, is that, "the labor of the manufacturer fixes and realizes itself in some particular subject or vendible commodity, which lasts for some time at least after that labor is past. It is, as it were, a certain quantity of labor stocked and stored up to be employed, if necessary upon some other occasion. . . . The labor of the menial servant, on the contrary, does not fix or realize itself in any particular subject or vendible commodity. His services generally perish in the very instant of their performance, and seldom leave any trace or value behind them, for which an equal quantity of services could afterwards be procured." [5]

In Smith's classification not only "menial servants" were unproductive (though not necessarily useless) labor: "The sovereign . . . with all the officers both of justice and war who serve under him, the whole army and navy are unproductive laborers; also—churchmen, lawyers, physicians, men of letters of all kinds: players, buffoons, musicians, opera singers, opera dancers, etc. . . . Like the declamation of the actor, the harangue of the orator, or the tune of the musician, the work of all of them perishes in the very instant of its production." [6] Thus Smith made tangibility with its associated quality of durability of the economic activity the criterion of productiveness. The continued viability of Smith's doctrine is illustrated by the fact that his distinction between material and nonmaterial goods, and the consequent productiveness or nonproductive-

---

[3] *Ibid.*, p. 18.
[4] Adam Smith, *The Wealth of Nations*, Modern Library ed., p. 314.
[5] *Ibid.*, pp. 314-15.
[6] *Ibid.*, p. 315.

ness of them, became part of the Marxian categories and found their way subsequently into modern Soviet concepts of national income accounting.[7]

It was actually Smith's greatest disciple on the Continent, J. B. Say, who saw Smith's error in this regard and who laid the basis for the modern concept of utilities. "Say had . . . recognized the claims of immaterial wealth alongside of material and he had employed the term 'services' in describing them. He held that the professor, the doctor and the actor had claims to be regarded as producers."[8] Gide and Rist tell us that the term "services" originated with J. B. Say in his *Traite d'Économie Politique*, written in 1803.

Alfred Marshall retained a part of the Smithian concept of perishability by remarking, "Services and other goods which pass out of existence in the same instant that they come into it are, of course, not part of the stock of wealth."[9] However, he goes on to state, "Man cannot create material things,"[10] implying that all productive activities consist of services applied to preexisting physical materials, and he sets out the currently generally accepted view concerning the essential unity of the productive process, as follows:

It is sometimes said that traders do not produce, that while the cabinet-maker produces furniture, the furniture dealer merely sells what is already produced. But there is no scientific foundation for this distinction. They both produce utilities and neither of them can do more: the furniture dealer moves and rearranges matter so as to make it more serviceable than it was before and the carpenter does nothing more. The sailor or the railway-man who carries coal above ground produces it, just as much as the miner who carries it underground; the dealer in fish helps to move on fish from where it is of

[7] Y. Rusanov, "Allocation of the Soviet Labor Force in Productive and Nonproductive Areas," *Soviet Review*, II (July, 1961).

[8] Charles Gide and Charles Rist, A *History of Economic Doctrines*, 1948 ed., p. 35.

[9] Alfred Marshall, *Principles of Economics*, 9th (variorum) ed., p. 56.

[10] *Ibid.*, p. 63.

comparatively little use to where it is of greater use, and the fisher-
man does no more.[11]

Toward a New View of Services

Despite Marshall's dictum to the effect that "there is not in
real life a clear line of division between things that are and are
not necessaries, or again between labor that is and is not productive," [12] much of the conventional thinking on the subject
of goods and services is based on the assumption of a clear-cut
distinction between the two. Can we in fact distinguish between a "pure good" and a "pure service"? The answer depends
on the particular case. For example, distinguishing between a
good and a service on the basis of tangibility certainly takes
one a long way and covers many if not most cases. Thus, a
"good" has specific physical dimensions whereas a "service" has
none, i.e., it is nonmaterial. Using this distinction, a pair of
shoes can clearly be classed as a good and a movie or a ball
game or a concert may be placed in the "service" category (entertainment). One author uses the apt term "experiential" to
apply to the latter group of services.[13] How shall we consider
a shoeshine or a haircut? Conventionally, these are classified
under the heading of "personal services," but in both cases
some physical alteration is associated with the service—the
appearance of both the shoes and the head is changed. Similarly, laundry and window-cleaning services involve physical
changes in the material cleaned. A key to this problem, and
perhaps to a more appropriate way of defining goods and services, is the ease with which one can separate the "good" from
the "service" it yields.

The utility of goods, like the utility of services, derives from

[11] *Ibid.*
[12] *Ibid.*, p. ix.
[13] Robert C. Judd, "The Case for Redefining Services," *Journal of Marketing*, XXVIII (January, 1964), 58–59.

the satisfactions that they can yield to the purchaser, be he producer or consumer. A pair of shoes can protect the consumer from injury and provide him with comfort. But the "service" which the shoe yields—protection and comfort— resides in the good, an item that can be produced, stored, and shipped. This is quite different from the haircut, where the service is inherent in the activity—it cannot be produced, stored, or shipped. Similarly, the song cannot be separated from the singer (or could not, before the technological advance of recording), or the dental service from the dentist. This basic characteristic of services, namely that they seem to "pass out of existence in the same instant that they come into it," explains in part why very little has been done in the further exploration of the services category; most of the economists' efforts have been devoted to classifying and refining the "goods" portion of total output.

In view of the even larger role that services have assumed in contemporary economic life, it is desirable to pursue, more systematically than has yet been pursued, the search for a classification system for services. But first a word by way of background of where we stand with respect to the classification of commodities.

The classic scheme of commodities classification was set forth by Professor Simon Kuznetz in his *Commodity Flow and Capital Formation,* published in 1938.[14] In that volume a basic twofold division of commodities into consumer goods and producer goods was presented, with three subdivisions under each, namely, perishable, semidurable, and durable. In turn, each of these subdivisions was viewed from the point of view of stage of production; from the unfinished raw materials to the finished product "at destination."

Much of this taxonomic scheme can and should be applied to services. The basic distinction between consumer services and

[14] Simon Kuznets, *Commodity Flow and Capital Formation,* I, 6.

producer services needs little elaboration. Those services which "at destination" are used by households or individuals fall clearly under the former, and those services used ultimately by business firms and other productive enterprises are included in the latter. This distinction underlies our later analysis. But the concept of durability in the context of services is one which, to our knowledge, has not been explored and which therefore requires elucidation.

First, with respect to consumer services, in what sense can we speak of services, as being perishable, semidurable, or durable? Obviously, the degree of durability is related to the time span over which the good or service is utilized. In the case of goods, Kuznetz listed under "perishable" those commodities "that without marked change and retaining their essential physical identity are ordinarily employed in their ultimate use less than six months."[15] The examples of such consumer perishables which he gave were bread and cigarettes. Without necessarily using the same time span as Kuznetz used for goods (i.e., perishable, less than six months; semidurable, six months to three years; durable, more than three years), we may nevertheless point out that such consumer services as a movie, a haircut, a ball game, or laundry service typically yield utility over a relatively short time span; that such consumer services as appliance repair and maintenance, some types of health services, some services of lawyers and accountants, can be thought of as being in the intermediate time span category—semidurable services, if you will; educational, engineering, and architectual services and particularly research may be placed in the longer-term or durable consumer services category. The essential point here is that tangibility or materiality is not a prerequisite for durability. Sir Hugh Carson, Professor of Interior Design at the Royal College of Art remarked recently that, "Choosing an architect for a university is just as important as

15 *Ibid.*, note.

choosing a professor. The former's mistakes will last longer and are more expensive to eradicate." [16]

Let us examine next the other major division, that is, producer services. What kinds of services are purchased by the firm and what are their durability characteristics? Again, much depends on the time span one wishes to use as the demarcation between perishable, semidurable, and durable. A service such as window cleaning, for example, may be regarded as a perishable producer service since the windows must be recleaned within a relatively short period of time. The same may be said of routine plant cleaning. In the semidurable category we might place many of the services provided by an advertising concern that is promoting the sale of a particular product, or of a lawyer who is dealing with negligence claims. Finally, among the durable producer services we would place those services which have to do with the long-range direction of the firm, such as those provided by business and management consulting firms and research and development projects. An institutional advertising campaign, or legal advice leading to a merger, would also fall into this category.

Needless to say, neither this services classification nor any goods classification is definitive; many goods and services are difficult to classify, and arbitrary decisions must occasionally be made. Nevertheless, it is important to note the parallelism between goods and services, and the fact that services can be analyzed in terms which have heretofore been exclusively reserved for goods. Furthermore, a typology of services along these lines would enable us to be more accurate in our national income accounting and in the concept and measurement of capital formation, for once the durability notion is applied to services, new and potentially fruitful analytical approaches come into view. We can now begin to think, for example, in terms of storability (e.g., data and programs on computer

[16] New York *Times,* March 18, 1965, p. E11.

tapes) postponability, obsolescence, inventory, and financing problems in the services areas. One of the most important applications of the durability of services concept is in the analysis of demand fluctuations over the business cycle. While we have not undertaken such a study in the present work, it would be highly instructive to determine whether, and how, the demand for services of different durabilities varies over the cycle. At a somewhat higher level of abstraction, the durability-of-services concept also has implications for the theory of interest and for what Becker [17] has called the theory of the allocation of time.

When one attempts to analyze the producer services sector, one is struck by the dearth of data. Neither private firms, nonprofit trade associations, nor government agencies provide adequate statistical coverage of this area. Perhaps this situation is due in part to the fact that we are still victims of the "conventional wisdom" which holds that investments consist solely of business spending for plant and equipment and which, in turn, largely rests on the older theories that goods are "productive" whereas "services" are not.

Producer Services and Current Economic Thinking

In sum, while the total output of our economy can be divided in one sense along the broad lines of goods and services, we have attempted to show that the division is not clear-cut. We have seen that the durable and nondurable characteristics used in the analysis of commodities has applicability to the services sector as well. Moreover, we believe that the distinction between consumer and producer goods will facilitate both the description and the analysis of an advanced economy, and, by way of contrast, should serve to illuminate some problems of developing economies as well.

Our view, then, is that the consumer-producer dichotomy

[17] Gary S. Becker, "A Theory of the Allocation of Time," *Economic Journal,* LXXV (September, 1965), 493–517.

with respect to goods can be applied to the services sphere. Consumer goods are defined as those satisfying a final demand, and producer goods as those entering into the further production of output. It follows therefore that producer services are in the nature of intermediate and not final outputs. This approach to producer services raises a whole host of questions, not all of which can be answered in this study. But it represents a first step toward a better understanding of the role of services in the economic process. It is interesting and encouraging to note that an important new stream in economic research focuses on investment in human resources in economic growth [18] and that this type of investigation runs parallel to our present study of producer services, i.e., the role of nonmaterial capital in the investment process. We hasten to point out, however, that the recent work on the role of the human factor in economic development has so far not resulted in any changes either in our conceptual national accounting framework or in the gathering and dissemination of statistical data on business or consumer spending for services.

It is easy to appreciate that a manufacturing firm which purchases the services of an economist, a market research agency, or a management consulting firm, may benefit therefrom more than from an equivalent investment in plant and equipment, in terms of an income stream over time. There is no theoretical justification for the view whether stated explicitly or, through neglect of the issue, implicitly, that business spending for such services does not constitute investment. The economist or the market researcher may be able to point to new avenues of activity open to the firm in much the same way and with the same lucrative potential as a new device developed by the firm's scientists and engineers. One business executive re-

[18] *Investment in Human Beings*, Supplement, *Journal of Political Economy*, LXX, No. 5 (October, 1962, Part 2), *passim*. See also the interesting communication of Lee R. Preston and E. C. Keachie, "Cost Functions and Progress Functions: An Integration," *American Economic Review*, LIV (March, 1964), 100–106.

cently expressed this thought in so many words: "Salmon [Kurt Salmon Associates, Inc., management consultants] saves me money. I look on his work as a piece of equipment, figuring out how much it will cost, how I will amortize it." [19]

As early as 1951, Joel Dean recognized "improvements in methods and know-how" as a distinct type of capital expenditure. He noted that, in substance, this "may involve investments in consulting services, technical education or interoffice rapport." [20] Moreover, and this is the crux of the matter, he stated that "capital expenditure should be defined in terms of economic behavior rather than in terms of accounting conventions or tax law." [21] Dean is aware that his "definition of outlays that budget as capital expenditures does not correspond well to the accounting distinction between capitalized and expended outlays." He further stated that "although we include most items capitalized by accountants, we also include some inportant expenditures that are usually expensed by accountants such as long term advertising, training and research. The disparity hinges largely on the tangibility of an asset rather than its economic nature, and contrasts the need for controls and conventions in accounting with the economist's intellectual license." [22]

Dean's views receive support in an important recent work by Fritz Machlup, who states, "When knowledge is produced in order that or in the expectation that as a result, the productivity of resources—human, natural or man-made—will increase in the foreseeable future, the production of knowledge can be regarded as an investment." [23] Of special interest to us is Machlup's discussion of producer services in particular:

[19] Statement of Mr. Joseph Zepshire, Executive Vice-President of a textile firm, quoted in, "Consultants: The Men Who Came to Dinner," by Walter Guzzardi, Jr., *Fortune*, LXXI (February, 1965), 236.

[20] Joel Dean, *Managerial Economics*, p. 601.

[21] *Ibid.*, p. 554.

[22] *Ibid.*, p. 555.

[23] Fritz Machlup, *The Production and Distribution of Knowledge in the United States*, p. 37.

. . . the services of certified public accountants, marketing research organizations and consulting engineers are sold almost entirely to business firms. Whether the firms buying these services use them for producing consumer goods or capital goods [durable producer goods] does not matter for our purposes; in either case, the production of knowledge serves in the current production of other things and the cost of the production of knowledge will be part of the cost of these other things, not a separate item in the national product, gross or net. The services of consulting engineers will perhaps be used more often in connection with new construction than with the current production of manufactured goods, and it might be interesting to see what portions of the investment in new plants are payments for knowledge produced in its planning and design. The services of architects are altogether of this sort; whether for industrial or residential construction, they furnish knowledge to be embodied in durable assets and the cost of this knowledge becomes part of the investment in fixed plant or dwellings.[24]

We need not agree with Machlup's contention that the work of market research organizations and consulting engineers should be considered only as part of current production. It was indicated earlier that such work often has long-range effects and should be considered a durable producer service. But the major point of the quotation is well taken, namely, that there is a definite service component in such an investment process. "We have often been shown," states Machlup, "the secular increase in the amount of capital per worker and the enormous rise of the use of machine-generated energy [horsepower] per worker. It would surely be interesting to see statistical evidence of the increase in the quantity of knowledge-producing labor per manual worker." [25]

Service Occupations

Some further preliminary distinctions and considerations should be mentioned here to provide a more adequate frame-

24 *Ibid.*, pp. 39–40.
25 *Ibid.*, p. 41.

work for the analysis which follows. Specifically, there is need to note certain trends in the types of workers, the types of firms, and the types of activities that different firms engage in which bear on the analysis of services in general and producer services in particular.

The past several decades have witnessed a marked increase in white collar workers relative to blue collar workers. This has been true even in the major goods producing sector of the economy, namely, manufacturing. The fact is that nonproduction (service) workers are just as important to the productive process as are production workers. Inadequate maintenance of the work environment (e.g., lighting, sanitation, air, water, safety procedures and devices) for instance, which may be considered to be in the nonproduction realm, can halt or interrupt the production process as much as a strike of production workers, or the breakdown of a piece of machinery or the use of defective materials. By the same token, faulty inventory accounting and forecasting techniques, poor management of the overall work flow, and the like may also result in the disorganization of the entire productive process.

The ratio of nonproduction workers to total employment within the manufacturing firm has been growing secularly due to a combination of internal and external factors. Internal need arises from the sheer fact of the firm's growth and the consequent necessity for record keeping, personnel work, and similar activities. External need for nonproduction workers arises from the requirements of government, fiscal, and regulatory agencies. By general agreement, production workers handle tools and equipment, leaving the nonproduction workers (e.g., white collar professional technical, administrative, and clerical personnel) to deal with the paper work, the work milieu, and "ideas." It is not surprising to learn, therefore, that even "within the manufacturing sector, the service or nonproduction workers' share of total employment increased from 7 percent in 1900 to 25 percent in 1962." [26]

But the foregoing statistical finding must be related to the changing structure of manufacturing concerns and the way they operate. Let us assume that a goods producing firm decides to contract out some of the nonproduction or services activities it had previously performed "in-house." This action does not reduce the aggregate nonproductive or services effort required to produce the final output; it simply changes the location and the group performing the activity. The internal function becomes external. The result is to cause the ratio of nonproduction workers to all workers in the firm to decline. However, if we include in our calculations the amounts of external services this firm purchases, then the total amount of nonproduction or services activity required for that firm's total output can be reconstituted.

The reverse process may also occur; namely, portions of a firm's manufacturing activity may be subcontracted, leading to a rise in its ratio of nonproduction employees to total employees. It is necessary only to note here how market practices affect the ratio of services workers to production workers, and to point out the pitfalls of assessing trends solely on an establishment or plant basis. Furthermore, in measuring job creation, we must be on guard not to count a transfer of activity as net growth. This caveat does not imply that the entire growth of producer services are transfers. A wide range of new services is being offered and an increased use of older services due to shifts in demand, price decreases, or quality increases is unquestionably occurring.

Our final comment concerns occupational differentiation within firms which supply services. A division can certainly be

[26] Daniel E. Diamond, "Changing Composition of the Labor Force—The Shift to Services: What Does It Mean?" in *Selected Readings in Employment and Manpower*, I, 109.

made between bookkeeping, clerical, and administrative personnel on the one hand and those who are more directly concerned with the final output. For example, a firm supplying legal services to other business firms employs clerical labor as well as lawyers, although the latter, of course, perform the basic work of the firm. While we noted earlier that nonproduction as well as production workers play essential parts in the output of commodities, the distinction between these two types of labor has been a useful analytic device. Hence, it may be well to find the equivalent in the services sector. Here, the labor input mix might more appropriately be described as "directly associated" or "indirectly associated," in terms of the end product. In the law firm example, all lawyers might be classed as personnel "directly associated" and all other personnel as "indirectly associated" with the final output.

The succeeding chapters represent a modest attempt to develop new knowledge about producer services, to estimate the factors underlying their growth, and in particular to probe their manpower dimensions. To the extent that these goals are approached and met, the basis will have been laid for the more systematic collection of data about this dynamic sector, for more probing analyses, and for a clarification of the directions of public policy.

Chapter II

THE SCALE OF PRODUCER SERVICES

Just as measurement is the foundation of science, so is classification the basis of measurement. The task of the present chapter is to assess the scale of producer services. A first step in such an effort is to set up an appropriate system of industry classification, with the recognition that any system will necessarily have some drawbacks. As E. A. G. Robinson has so aptly pointed out, "Industries as such have no identity. They are simply a classification of firms which may for the moment be convenient. A change of technique and or organization may require a new classification and a new industry." [1]

While some system of classification is necessary if the economy is to be studied, every system has perforce a retrospective orientation. It starts from conditions that once existed and that, at least in part, no longer exist. At various stages in economic development, new activities or products must be noted, declining ones eliminated, and existing output distinguished on the basis of new technology or new industrial organization. Yet, some categories remain applicable. For instance, despite dynamic changes in steel technology from Bessemer to open-hearth to oxygen furnace, basic statistics on the steel industry are still gathered and have validity. The classification problem is basically one of designing appropriate categories to collect the relevant data in order to illuminate the dynamics of economic change.

A brief overview of the changing concepts and scope of suc-

[1] E. A. G. Robinson, *The Structure of Competitive Industry*, p. 13.

cessive Censuses will help illustrate this critical problem. The first and second Censuses, for example (1790 and 1800), were concerned solely with age, sex, and color of the population. In the third Census (1810), "an attempt was made for the first time to gather industrial statistics." [2] At that time, the major divisions of economic activity for which information was sought were agriculture, commerce, navigation, and the fisheries. Even at this early stage of our economic development, a classification problem arose which necessitated a separate estimate of "the goods made in the U.S. which are of a doubtful nature in relation to their character as *manufactures* or agricultural." [3]

As the economy developed, the need for more comprehensive data became manifest as shown by the Census of 1840, which sought such "information in relation to mines, agriculture, commerce, manufacture and schools as will exhibit a full view of the pursuits, industry, education and resources of this country." [4]

The influence of analytical concepts may be observed from the language used in one of the schedules of the 1850 Census, which "was intended to apply to all forms of *productive* industry including manufacture, mining and the fisheries and all kinds of mercantile, commercial or trading business." (Italics added.) The inference, of course, was that the latter three were "nonproductive."

Reflecting the rapid growth in total output and the increasing diversification of the economy in the post-Civil War period, the Census of 1880 included information on the financial and business operations of life and fire and marine insurance companies and associations, as well as express and telegraph companies.

This thumbnail sketch of changes in the industry classifications used by the Census in the last century has two morals. It

[2] Carroll D. Wright, *The History and Growth of the U.S. Census,* pp. 21–22.
[3] *Ibid.,* p. 24 (emphasis in original).
[4] *Ibid.,* p. 33.

indicates the need for changes in categories to reflect changes in the economy; and it underscores, if only implicitly, that the empirical investigator is largely confined to the categories in use at his point in time.

Goods Industries Versus Services Industries

The first and most general question with which we are concerned is whether the output of a group of industries is to be viewed as the output of goods or of services. Once this distinction has been made, we can proceed to the central discussion of the subcategories of the services sector.

Starting with the Standard Industrial Classification (SIC) used in the Census, there is developed below a regrouping based on the following criteria:

All economic activities which result in the transformation of some basic raw material into a different (and presumably more useful) form should be placed in the output-of-goods category. Thus, agricultural and nonagricultural outputs are similar from this point of view. Fishing, dairying, and meat production would all be subsumed under agriculture.

The output-of-goods classification would apply up to that stage in the productive process where a final end-product appears—e.g., an orange, an automobile, a printing press—and would therefore cover all intermediate products.

Somewhat arbitrarily, steam, electric, and gas plants would be classified with the output-of-goods sector even though these activities involve the transformation of fuels into other forms of energy. However, steam, electricity, and gas are very much like goods in that they have specific physical characteristics which enable their production to be closely controlled in quantity and quality.[5]

[5] David C. Cates in "The Service Industries: Classification for Investors," *Commercial and Financial Chronicle,* November 23, 1961, p. 26, states: "The F.P.C. reflected this ambiguity [i.e., between goods and services] by shifting

All economic activities which commence with a preexisting product and merely change its location (transportation) or in minor ways its physical appearance (packaging), or are concerned with its eventual disposition (wholesale and retail trade), are classified in the output-of-services category. Communications—that is to say, those firms which derive revenues from the provision of communication facilities—will likewise be classified as services.

The fields of banking, real estate, insurance, and investment all provide intangible utilities and therefore belong under the services rubric.

Construction (of buildings, roads, etc.) is clearly in the output-of-goods sector. Closely allied to this field are wrecking companies, which engage in the destruction of buildings and equipment. Their activities could conceivably be classified as services, but with some degree of arbitrariness we shall place them in the goods sector.

The activities of recreation, education, health, law, religion, public administration, accounting, philanthropy, research, and the like, are not directly associated with the output of physical commodities, hence they can all be safely included in the services sector.

The following category scheme (using SIC terminology) sets forth schematically the principal subdivisions under goods and services output, in accordance with the criteria outlined above.[6]

---

part of its gas regulatory approach from a service orientation [rate of return] to a commodity orientation [area pricing]. As for electricity, I think it is merely obsolete philosophy that refuses to define it as a manufactured good. In every respect other than physical tangibility, it meets the earmarks of manufacture, i.e., continuous processing of a transportable commodity."

[6] It might be useful to compare the classification system proposed here with that of the United Nations' *International Standard Industrial Classification of All Economic Activities;* and with that employed for specific analytic purposes by Victor R. Fuchs in *Productivity Trends in the Goods and Service Sector, 1929–1961: A Preliminary Survey.*

I. Goods Output

Division A—Agriculture, forestry, and fisheries

Division B—Mining

Division C—Contract construction

Division D—Manufacturing

Division E—Only the electric and gas components of the general group (transportation, communication, electric, gas, and sanitary services)

II. Services Output

Division E—Transportation, communication, electric, gas, and sanitary services (all groups with the exceptions of those mentioned under I-E above)

Division F—Wholesale and retail trade

Division G—Finance, insurance, and real estate

Division H—Services

Division I—Government

The foregoing classification system provides us with a springboard for our major effort, which is to gain new understanding of the scale and scope of the producer services segment of the economy.

Statistical Profile of the Producer Services Sector

The problems involved in sharply distinguishing producer from consumer services were well stated by Professor Stigler: [7]

The industries that provide services to the business community do not form a category wholly distinct from those providing services to consumers; there is indeed, a fairly continuous array of industries between the limits. At one extreme, service industries, such as the consulting construction engineers serve only business; in the middle of the array, independent lawyers receive approximately equal shares of income from business and nonbusiness clients; and at the other extreme, teachers serve individuals in their nonbusiness capacity. Enough important industries fall in the category of those serving chiefly business, however, to justify separate discussion.

One can point out, with respect to the above quotation, that

[7] George J. Stigler, *Trends in Employment in the Service Industries*, p. 138.

consulting construction engineers serve not only business but government and nonprofit organizations as well, and that teachers are sometimes employed by business firms to provide on-the-job training, but this would not vitiate Stigler's central proposition, which is that this sector of our economy consists of business firms whose output is purchased primarily by other business firms rather than by individual consumers as final demand. The determination of the dimensions of this sector is our task at this point, and for this purpose we employ two basic economic yardsticks—those of employment and of income.

Table 1

EMPLOYMENT IN PRODUCER SERVICES, 1950 AND 1960

Industry	1950	1960	Percent Change
	(*thousands of persons*)		*1950–1960*
Transportation (3/4)[a]	2,176	2,016	− 7.4
Communications (1/4)	350	406	+ 16.0
Wholesale trade	2,143	2,425	+ 13.2
Finance, insurance, and real estate (1/2)	945	1,325	+ 40.2
Advertising	109	128	+ 17.4
Miscellaneous business services	242	622	+ 157.0
Industrial medical	n.a.	n.a.	
Legal (1/2)	115	140	+ 21.7
Engineering and architectural (9/10)	75	179	+ 138.6
Accounting, auditing, and bookkeeping (9/10)	91	140	+ 53.8
Miscellaneous professional services (3/4)	51	79	+ 54.9
Government [b] (1/3)	731	1,064	+ 45.6
Total producer services	7,028	8,524	+ 21.3
Total all industries	56,097	64,647	+ 15.2
Producer services as percent of total	12.5	13.2	

N.a.: not available.

[a] Ratios in parentheses indicate proportion of total employment allocated to producer services. See text for explanation. Adjusted for Alaska and Hawaii.

Source: U.S. Department of Commerce, Bureau of the Census, *U.S. Census of Population, 1950* and *1960.*

Table 1 provides the basic list of industries which we classified as producer services, together with their employment figures for 1950 and 1960. Figures for this breakdown are not available from Census data before 1950. Many, if not all, of these industries serve business firms and individuals, as well as government and nonprofit organizations. It is also true that when these firms report their employment figures, they do not differentiate between the proportions of their labor force engaged in producer services and those devoted primarily to services for the consumer. It is therefore necessary to adopt an estimating procedure in order to develop a total for workers engaged in producer services. We have estimated employment from detailed breakdowns of revenue which are more readily obtainable. However, even data of this sort are not available for many industries. When such revenue data were not available, other bases were used to make an estimate of the proportion of the labor force involved in producer services. Moreover, we have employed the simplifying assumption that the ratios of producer services to total employment were unchanged between 1950 and 1960. The resulting table must therefore be viewed as a first approximation, nothing more.

The ratios in the parentheses following many of the industries in Table 1 indicate the proportion of their total employment which we have allocated to producer services. In the case of transportation, for instance, we have reasoned that railroad transportation, motor freight, warehousing, water transportation, air transportation, pipelines, are overwhelmingly devoted to business services. The 3/4 ratio which we have used is also guided, in part, by the interindustry input-output tables of the U. S. Department of Commerce, which indicate that 74.6 percent of the output of the transportation industry is sold to "intermediate users" and to other nonconsumer components of "final demand." [8]

[8] Morris P. Goldman, Martin L. Marimont, and Beatrice U. Vaccara, "The Interindustry Structure of the United States," *Survey of Current Business*, XLIV (November, 1964), 10–29.

In the communications industries, the bulk of revenues are derived from telephone and telegraph service. Although there are roughly twice as many resident (i.e., nonbusiness) as business telephones, the average business phone bill is at least twice that of the average nonbusiness consumer phone bill which suggests that a 50-50 distribution is reasonable. Almost all radio and television broadcasting revenues are derived from the sale of "time" to business firms. Referring again to the Commerce Department's interindustry tables, we find that 57.9 percent of the communications industry's output (exclusive of radio and television broadcasting) is sold to intermediate users. For the sake of simplicity and because we desire to avoid exaggerating the size of producer services, we have used a ratio of 1/2.

Similar problems of allocation arise in connection with finance, insurance, and real estate. The major portion of bank revenues, for instance, is derived from their loan portfolio, a breakdown of which yields an approximately equal division between loans to consumers and loans to business firms, although the number of employees required to service the consumer portion is probably higher. The growth of group insurance, which is sold mainly to business firms, and business transactions in real estate, indicates the growing importance of revenue derived from sales to business firms. Turning to the input-output tables, we find a separation of our single category into two parts. The first part, finance and insurance, shows that 55.4 percent of the output is sold to intermediate users, and the second "industry," real estate and rental, is more consumer oriented since only 35.5 percent of its output is sold to business firms or government. Here, therefore, a 50 percent weight for the group as a whole appears to be warranted.

The most difficult conceptual and statistical problems associated with the task of allocating manpower between producer and consumer services arise with respect to government operations. There is very little in the literature to which one can refer for illumination on this point. Stigler, for example, cited a 1938 study by Nelson and Jackson in which it is estimated that 32 percent of all government services were rendered to business.[9] Below is an illustration of the manner in which we arrived at the ratio used herein. A percent distribution of all public employees by function for 1960 is shown in column 1:

	(1)	(2)
National defense	11.9	6.0
Postal service	6.4	4.2
Education	33.3	3.0
Highways	6.1	4.0
Health and hospitals	9.7	0.0
Police protection	4.1	2.0
Natural resources	3.7	3.6
General control	6.6	3.3
All other	18.2	9.1
Total	100.0	35.2

Source of column 1: Bureau of the Census, *State Distribution of Public Employment in 1960*, p. 7.

The figures in column 2 are largely judgmental and are derived from postulates such as that defense and police functions should be allocated on a 50-50 basis (following Nelson and Jackson); that roughly 2/3 of the mail handled is of a business nature; that 9/10 of education is consumer oriented; that the great bulk of natural resource projects are direct aids to producers (e.g., to farmers); and that all other functions are equally divided in their direct impact on consumers and producers. Obviously, these postulates may all be contested, and hopefully the ratios may be rendered more precise by additional detailed studies in this area. For the present purposes our view is that a 1/3 ratio of public employment is representa-

[9] R. W. Nelson and Donald Jackson, "Allocation of Benefits from Government Expenditures," in *Studies in Income and Wealth*, II, 317–27 (cited in Stigler, p. 142).

tive of the government manpower effort devoted to serving firms and/or individuals in their capacities as producers. In order to simplify subsequent calculations, we have made the further assumption that the ratios were the same for 1950 and 1960.

The revenues of accounting, auditing, and bookkeeping services firms are overwhelmingly derived from sales to business, which is the basis for the 9/10 ratio. In the case of legal services, a significant amount of legal work involves negligence, domestic, and estate cases—all individual consumer-oriented—but in our view, taking account of the continuing high volume of corporate and business legal work justifies the 50-50 estimate.

While the limitations of the estimation procedures employed here must be kept in mind, the statistical profile developed indicates that in 1960 about 8½ million workers, or a little more than 13 percent of the total labor force, were engaged in enterprises producing services for other businesses and for non-profit and government institutions. Moreover, while total employment rose by 15.2 percent during the decade of the 1950s, employment in producer services increased some 21.3 percent. This 21 percent increase in total employment in producer services conceals a great deal of variation among the component industries, ranging from a decline of about 7 percent in transportation to a 157 percent increase in the "miscellaneous business services" category.

Another way of measuring the role of producer services in the economy is to determine the absolute and relative amounts of national income (i.e., payments to the factors of production) that originate in this segment. Table 2 sets out the relevant data, using much the same assumptions, definitions, and restrictions as were employed in constructing Table 1. In addition, another source of difficulty is introduced by not adjusting for price changes between 1950 and 1960. It is interesting to

Table 2

NATIONAL INCOME ORIGINATING IN SELECTED PRODUCER
SERVICES, 1950 AND 1960

Industry	1950	1960	Percent Change 1950–1960
	(millions of dollars)		
Transportation (3/4) [a]	9,957	13,431	+ 34.9
Communications (1/2)	3,599	8,404	+ 134.0
Wholesale trade	13,682	23,875	+ 74.5
Finance, insurance, and real estate (1/2)	10,894	21,293	+ 95.5
Business services, n.e.c.	2,097	6,044	+ 188.0
Legal services (1/2)	670	1,333	+ 99.0
Engineering (9/10)	658	2,100	+ 219.0
Government (1/3)	7,829	17,509	+ 123.6
Total producer services	49,386	93,989	+ 90.3
Total national income	241,876	414,497	+ 71.4
Producer services as % of total national income	20.4	22.7	

N.e.c.: not elsewhere classified.

[a] See pp. 23–26 for explanation of parentheses.

Sources: U.S. Department of Commerce, Office of Business Economics, *U.S. Income and Output,* pp. 130–31; and *Survey of Current Business,* July, 1964, p. 13.

note, that from the data in both tables, in 1960 the producer services segment may have accounted for about 13 percent of total employment, but for almost 23 percent of total income. From Table 3 we find that the major component of the services category—consumer services—accounted for about 49 percent of total employment but only 37 percent of total income. It should be noted that some additional qualifications are attached to the use of the "income originating" data, namely that the real estate subgroup includes imputed income from owner-occupied dwellings and that the government figures do not include a return to capital.

Relative changes in income among the individual industrial components are shown in Table 4. The figures appearing in the latter table may be compared with those of employment distribution in Table 5. In terms of employment, the most im-

Table 3

CHANGES IN EMPLOYMENT AND INCOME IN SERVICES, 1950 AND 1960

Category	Employment			Income		
	1950	*1960*	*Percent Change 1950– 1960*	*1950*	*1960*	*Percent Change 1950– 1960*
	(millions of persons)			*(millions of dollars)*		
Consumer services	26.0	31.9	+ 22.7	81.6	153.0	+ 87.5
Producer services	7.0	8.5	+ 21.3	49.4	94.0	+ 90.3
All services	33.0	40.4	+ 22.4	131.0	247.0	+ 89.0
All goods and services	56.0	65.0	+ 15.2	242.0	414.0	+ 71.0
			Ratios			
Consumer services as % of all services	78.8	79.0		62.3	61.9	
Producer services as % of all services	21.2	21.0		37.7	38.1	
Consumer services as % of total	47.3	49.0		33.7	37.0	
Producer services as % of total	12.5	13.1		20.4	22.7	
All services as % of total	58.9	62.2		54.0	59.0	

Totals may not add to 100 due to rounding.
Sources: Same as for Tables 1 and 2.

Table 4

PERCENTAGE DISTRIBUTION OF NATIONAL INCOME ORIGINATING IN PRODUCER SERVICES, 1950 AND 1960

Industry	*1950*	*1960*
Transportation	20.2	14.3
Communications	7.3	8.9
Wholesale trade	27.7	25.4
Finance, insurance, and real estate	22.1	22.7
Business services, n.e.c.	4.3	6.4
Legal	1.4	1.4
Engineering	1.3	2.2
Government	15.9	18.6
Total producer services	100.0	100.0

N.e.c.: not elsewhere classified.
Totals may not add to 100 due to rounding.
Sources: Same as for Table 2.

Table 5

PERCENTAGE DISTRIBUTION OF EMPLOYMENT
IN PRODUCER SERVICES,
1950 AND 1960

	Percent of Total Employment	
Industry	1950	1960
Transportation	21.0	23.7
Communications	5.0	4.8
Wholesale trade	30.5	28.4
Finance, insurance, and real estate	13.4	15.5
Advertising	1.6	1.5
Miscellaneous business services	3.4	7.3
Legal	1.6	1.6
Engineering	1.1	2.1
Accounting, auditing, etc.	1.3	1.6
Miscellaneous professional services	.7	.9
Government	10.4	12.5
Total producer services	100.0	100.0

Totals may not add to 100 due to rounding.
Source: Same as for Table 1.

portant subgroups within the producer services segment in 1950 were (in order of importance) wholesale trade, transportation, finance, and government. In 1960, the same four groups were dominant, but wholesale trade and transportation reversed rankings and they also decreased in intrasectoral importance. In terms of the income distribution, wholesale trade, finance, transportation, and government occupied the first four ranks in 1950. In 1960, the first two subgroups retained their relative importance, but government now exceeded transportation.

A further comparison of intrasectoral employment and income shifts over the 1950–1960 decade yields some interesting observations. The miscellaneous business and engineering subgroups show rapid (defined here as over 100 percent) employment as well as rapid income growth over the decade. Transportation, on the other hand, exhibited an actual decline in employment as well as the smallest growth in income. Industries which registered a relatively low growth in employment (all below 100 percent) but a relatively substantial growth in income were communications, legal services, government, and finance. Wholesale trade recorded only a 13.2 percent increase in employment but a 74.5 percent increase in income.

Taking the producer services segment as a whole, the data indicate that it has grown in importance relative to the entire economy in the decadal period. In 1960, employment in this area constituted 13.2 percent of total employment, whereas in 1950 the comparable figure was 12.5 percent. In terms of income originating in producer services, the 1960 ratio of producer services to total income was 22.7 percent, compared with a 20.4 percent ratio for 1950. Some of the reasons for this shift as well as the implications thereof are explored in subsequent chapters.

A summary showing changes in employment and income in the entire services area and in the producer services segment during the decade of the 1950s is presented in Table 3. Several suggestive points emerge. Whereas total employment increased by 15.2 percent between 1950 and 1960, employment in services as a whole rose by 22.4 percent. If the services sector is divided between consumer services and producer services, the former shows a 22.7 percent and the latter a 21.3 percent increase in employment. While total national income increased by 71.0 percent, income in the entire services sector rose by 89.0 percent, and by 87.5 and 90.3 percent in consumer and producer services, respectively.

These data lead us to infer that both in terms of employment and in terms of income, growth rates in the services were significantly higher than in the economy as a whole. To the extent that the general estimating procedures are valid, growth rates in the producer and the consumer services sectors were roughly equivalent. It should be pointed out, however, that the producer services sector included some large but relatively slow-moving components such as transportation, wholesale trade, and government. The more dynamic elements in the producer services are to be found in the smaller segments such as the miscellaneous business services group, the engineering and architectural services, and miscellaneous professional services. The latter group includes such producer services as actuarial bureaus, consulting chemists, meteorological services, and scientific and statistical research agencies.

Dynamic Producer Services

Detailed analyses of several of the larger industries involved in producer services have been available for some time. In addition to Stigler's work, reference should be made to the studies by Harold Barger on transportation and distribution, Solomon Fabricant on government employment, Raymond Goldsmith on financial intermediaries, and Thor Hultgren on transportation.[10] The present monograph focuses specifically on some of the more dynamic components, and in particular on the group labeled "miscellaneous business services." This group has been singled out for a variety of reasons. First, as noted above, it is the most rapidly growing cluster of producer services industries and a detailed analysis of its pattern of growth may shed new light on the segment as a whole. Second, this group has not been studied intensively. Third, the manpower employed by industries within it is highly varied, ranging, for example, from less than one percent of all employees in building maintenance who are college graduates to a high of about 80 percent in management consulting. Hence, these industries provide an excellent opportunity to review the interrelating factors in a rapidly growing segment of the economy

[10] Harold Barger, *Distribution's Place in the American Economy Since 1863*, and *The Transportation Industries, 1889–1946: a Study of Output, Employment and Productivity*; Solomon Fabricant, *The Trend of Government Activity in the United States Since 1900*; Raymond W. Goldsmith, *Financial Intermediaries in the American Economy Since 1900*; Thor Hultgren, *American Transportation in Prosperity and Depression*. All are publications of the National Bureau of Economic Research (NBER). See also NBER *Annual Report for 1955*.

and the use which it makes of different types of manpower resources.

Not only has this cluster of producer services shown rapid growth over the 1950–1960 period, but the secular trend is equally impressive. Earlier data, roughly comparable though not based on the Census, show an increase in employment in "business services" of 254 percent between 1929 and 1957, whereas aggregate employment rose 37 percent over the same period.[11] We are dealing here with what is clearly a long-term growth pattern.

The heterogeneity of the "miscellaneous business services" group may be appreciated from a listing of its main subdivisions in the Bureau of the Census' *Classified Index of Occupations and Industries.*[12] Approximately 540 different types of producer services are listed, including such diverse activities as addressing service, building maintenance service, corporation organizers, drafting service, executive placement service, food consultant service, grain sampling, hotel employment agency, industrial designing of machinery, jet propulsion laboratory, labor conciliation service (nongovernmental), management consulting service, news syndicate, office cleaning service, payroll service, radiation laboratory, sales engineers, translation service, and window dressing service.

Information on some of these firms is provided by the *Census of Business,* and Table 6 shows a sampling of selected producer services, together with the number of establishments and employment in each from 1958 to 1963—the last two such Censuses.

While total nonagricultural employment rose by 10.3 percent between 1958 and 1963,[13] this rate was exceeded by each

11 U.S. Department of Labor, Bureau of Labor Statistics, *Employment and Earnings Statistics for the United States, 1909–64.*

12 U.S. Department of Commerce, Bureau of the Census, *Census of Population, 1960: Classified Index of Occupations and Industries,* pp. 360–64.

13 U.S. Department of Commerce, Bureau of the Census, *Historical Statistics of the United States, Colonial Times to 1957,* pp. 70 and 518.

Table 6

SELECTED PRODUCER SERVICES WITH HIGH EMPLOYMENT
GROWTH RATES, 1958 AND 1963

Producer Services	Number of Establishments		Percent Change	Paid Employees (work week ended nearest Nov. 15)		Percent Change
	1958	1963		1958	1963	
Direct mail advertising; duplicating, copying, and steno	9,880	13,932	+ 41.0	40,698	56,027	+ 37.7
Services to dwellings and other buildings	17,460	25,893	+ 48.3	91,127	152,756	+ 67.6
Research, development laboratories	1,043	1,540	+ 47.7	36,309	61,136	+ 68.4
Testing laboratories	960	1,549	+ 61.4	9,747	15,197	+ 55.9
Business, management consulting	12,765	20,879	+ 63.6	46,805	78,003	+ 66.7
Detective agencies, protective	2,831	3,644	+ 28.7	42,145	66,994	+ 59.0
Equipment rental	5,329	8,903	+ 67.1	20.057	31,711	+ 58.1
Coin-operated machine rental, repair	221	438	+ 98.2	476	926	+ 94.5
Photofinishing laboratories	1,907	2,639	+ 38.4	19,727	25,099	+ 27.2
Interior decorating	4,191	4,475	+ 6.7	2,278	3,711	+ 62.9
Sign painting shops	7,110	7,093	− .02	5,037	6,231	+ 23.7
Auctioneers' establishments (service only)	2,069	2,343	+ 13.2	1,842	2,636	+ 43.1
Telephone answering	1,656	2,513	+ 51.8	9,408	15,807	+ 68.0
Water softening	1,298	1,773	+ 36.6	4,568	6,564	+ 43.7
Supplying temporary office help for other businesses	n.a.	816			42,745	
Supplying temporary help except office, for other businesses	n.a.	443			17,637	

N.a.: not available.
Source: Adapted from U.S. Department of Commerce, Bureau of the Census, *Census of Business, 1958,* Vol. V, *Selected Services,* and *Census of Business, 1963, Selected Services, United States Summary.*

of the businesses listed, many by wide margins. Although the time period is a relatively short one, and some of the base figures are small, support is nevertheless given to the thesis that the area of producer services is one of expanding employment.

These diverse activities obviously differ not only with respect to the type of labor employed, but also by size of the average firm, revenues, market structure, and types of customers. The *1963 Census of Business* indicates that there are over 146,000 establishments in this area, employing nearly 876,000 workers.[14] Despite this diversity, there are two factors which most of these firms have in common; namely, their output is sold primarily to other business firms, and the latter typically possess a considerable latitude on the question whether to perform the function themselves or to contract it out. The next chapter addresses itself to the determinants of demand for business services as reflected by firms and organizations that purchase such services rather than provide them on their own account.

[14] U.S. Department of Commerce, Bureau of the Census, *Census of Business, 1963, Selected Services, United States Summary.*

Chapter III

THE DEMAND FOR PRODUCER SERVICES

Any portion of the economy that accounts for more than 8.5 million workers is worthy of detailed study. While we noted in the previous chapter that the older, larger service industries such as transportation, trade, and government have been subjected to careful analysis, it is correct to say that economists have for the most part neglected the service sector as a field of continuing investigation. Most of economic theory is derived from investigations into the classic prototype of industrialization—the manufacturing concern.

The present chapter seeks to isolate and to analyze the major determinants of the demand for external services on the part of the firm, that is to say, those services which a firm purchases from other, independent firms. Elucidation of these factors is undertaken through a brief survey of the literature on the demand for producer services as well as by reference to specific examples of the demand for such services by enterprises in the private, nonprofit, and government sectors of the economy. In addition, some quantitative evidence is presented and some qualitative judgments are assayed, which have a bearing on the future demand for external producer services.

Despite the fact that economists have used the principles of economies of scale to explain the inner momentum to economic growth, they have generally failed to apply these principles to the output of producer services; at least they have failed to pay much attention to the rapid growth of the new types of producer services.

Types of Producer Services

One approach to the discussion of demand for producer services is to set out an array of those which are actually purchased by business firms. In our first case study, a large retail department store in the City of New York prepared such a list at our request. In brief, this store identified the following 34 specific types of services bought in the market rather than performed on its own account.

Advertising
Air conditioning and filter
  maintenance
Architectural
Auditing
Business machine maintenance
Buying offices
Cleaning (night and day)
Customs brokerage
Data processing
Door front and brass maintenance
Elevator and escalator maintenance
Engineering
Entrance and sprinkler protection
Fashion model agencies
Food service for employees
Freight consolidation
General maintenance

Interior design
Labor relations
Legal
Mail and messenger
Market research
Medical
Muzak
Personnel checking
Protection (uniformed guards)
Public relations
Real estate
Sign maintenance
Tailoring
Trash and waste paper removal
Truck maintenance
Utility consultant
Water treatment

The diversity of these services as represented by the demand of a single enterprise has led us to develop the category scheme on page 37 to facilitate description and analysis. Using, as a point of departure, the distinctions introduced in Chapter I concerning the durability of services, this schematization has made a gross distinction between those which are used primarily to support policy making decisions and those more directly involved in administration—that is to say, routine operations. For the most part, the former have more of the characteristics of durable and semidurable services; the latter are largely perishable.

A FUNCTIONAL CLASSIFICATION OF PRODUCER SERVICES

POLICY-MAKING

Current Problems	*Longer-Range Planning*
Banking, insurance, and real estate advisors	Business management consulting services
Legal problems	Economic and market research
Personnel and labor relations consultants	Research development laboratories
Systems analysts	Testing laboratories

ADMINISTRATIVE

Production-Related	*Nonproduction*
Armored car services	Advertising
Detectives, protective services	Bookkeeping, accounting, etc.
Equipment rental	Coin-operated machine rental
Freight forwarding	Credit bureaus and collection agencies
Photofinishing laboratories	Direct mail advertising
Safety inspectors	Duplicating, copying, and stenographic services
Services to dwellings and other buildings	News syndication
Testing laboratories	Private employment agencies
	Public relations services
	Routine data processing
	Telephone answering

Determinants of Demand

With this category scheme before us, we are in a position to explore the principal determinants underlying the demand for producer services. Some of the following points are derived from the conventional model of the profit maximizing firm, while others are in the realm of what might be termed nonmarket-oriented or institutional behavior.

The first determinant to be considered is the desire to produce the existing level of output at a lower cost. Basic to the use of external services is the question of whether a specific function (e.g., general maintenance) can be performed at lower cost, with no loss in quality, by an outside agency. Where a job has been "contracted out," the firm has usually been convinced by cost comparisons that the work can be performed at a cost saving. Parenthetically, a major activity of firms selling services to other firms involves the preparation of "proposals" which specify the quantity, quality, and cost of the work to be done relative to the current cost of the operation. In their survey of the contracting-out process, Chandler and Sayles found that of all the reasons given by management, cost was the controlling factor most frequently cited.[1]

The usual explanation of the source of the saving is the greater productivity of the external labor force, which is at once more specialized and more closely supervised. In addition, important economies can also be realized by the service-selling firm through the purchasing of materials (e.g., discounts on bulk purchases) and through the improved scheduling of its labor force. In essence, we have operating here the basic principle of comparative advantage, whereby a firm will purchase services from other firms which may have absolute and/or relative advantages over itself in the performance of a specified function.

In the nonprofit and government sectors, the use of external services stems both from the need to increase general operational efficiency and the desire to escape from personnel constraints. As an example of the former, there are listed below the types of external services purchased by a medium sized, 268-bed capacity, voluntary hospital in Nassau County, New York:

> Laundry service
> Diaper service
> Machine processing of payroll
> Window cleaning
> Elevator maintenance
> Typewriter and business machine maintenance
> Legal services

[1] Margaret Chandler and Leonard Sayles, *Contracting-out, A Study in Management Decision Making*, p. 24.

Statistical services

Recorded background music

An illustration of the difference in the use of external services between the case of this hospital and that of the department store mentioned earlier, is the fact that "general maintenance," which appears on the store's list, is absent from that of the hospital. The reason is that in the latter case infection control is high on the list of priorities, and hospital administrators are loath to entrust this function to an outside firm. The same reasoning holds to a somewhat lesser extent with respect to the provision of food services and laundry.

In addition to the external services purchased by this hospital—a list which is probably typical for hospitals of this size—larger hospitals are also likely to employ the services of outside consultants or consulting firms on a periodic, if not continuing, basis. In one large voluntary hospital in the City of New York, consultants have been used more or less continuously in such areas as long-range planning, efficient integration of personnel, medical staff relations, board of trustees organization, and labor relations.

One reason hospitals in the past have not usually been large users of outside services is their concern with the quality of their output, namely patient care. Recourse to external services represents some degree of loss of control by the hospital administrator over a complex and sensitive type of enterprise. However, new trends are discernible. The steady and substantial increase in hospital wage levels as well as the rising costs of supplies and equipment have resulted in rapidly increasing charges to the patient. This in turn has caused growing concern not only to patients, but to the so-called third parties (e.g., insurance carriers, trade unions) as well as to legislators and administrators of state insurance funds. The pressures to cut or at least hold costs in check are intensifying, and even conservative hospital managements are giving increasing thought to ways in which this may be done, including greater recourse to external services.

An examination of the practices of a county personnel office in the State of New York was undertaken in order to determine the rationale for the use of external services by government units. Though not representative of other types of government organizations, the following kinds of external services were utilized in this particular unit.

> School bus transportation
> Maintenance of public buildings
> Food service
> Interior and exterior painting
> Engineering firms, designers, and surveyors
> Meteorological service
> Management consultants

Government officials who make decisions concerning the use of external services are under constraints not unlike those faced by their counterparts in the private and nonprofit sectors. The scrutiny of operating budgets by various taxpayer groups often requires the government officials to justify his utilizing external services rather than employing civil service workers to perform the same tasks. Pressures of an opposite sort are often exerted upon him by unions and other interest groups which desire the greater use of external services in order to maximize the employment and incomes of their own members. Hence, cost calculations, which are understood by all groups, must play a strategic role in decisions to use external services by government "firms."

A second determinant of the demand for external services, closely related to the first, is the desire to increase the quantity or quality of the output produced by currently employed resources.

The pursuit of this goal may entail the hiring of a packaging expert with the aim of making the company's product more attractive to consumers, or the use of a market research agency to determine whether a product should be altered to take account of changes in consumer preferences or whether a new product should in fact be produced and marketed.

The market research example can prove illuminating in the context of the present discussion, since it has been pointed out [2] that even though a firm may have its own market research department, the use of external market research agencies provides the following advantages: they are able to handle unusually large jobs, for which the company's own department is usually not adequately staffed or equipped, and in so doing they eliminate the costly and burdensome task of hiring a temporary staff; for the average-sized company, the professional, outside agency can provide a large field interviewing group at a saving in cost; such an agency possesses specialized skills not generally available among an in-house research department; and the use of such an outside agency is indicated when the company prefers to remain anonymous with respect to the interviewing or when it desires an independent check on one of its internal departments.

A third motive for using external business services is the desire of a firm to eliminate what might be termed troublesome functions, such as staffing low status jobs, dealing with complex jurisdictional or other problems in union-management relations, or coping with irregular work schedules.

Problems such as these have proved to be of considerable importance to many managements. Where a firm has to deal with several different unions, as in the construction and maintenance fields, it is often desirable to shift this burden to an individual or group experienced in such matters. Certain disagreeable functions—such as plant or office cleaning—frequently lead to tensions when performed by its regular work

[2] National Industrial Conference Board (NICB), *Studies in Business Policy*, No. 72: *Marketing Business and Commercial Research in Industry*.

force. Hence, by contracting out and assuming no reduction in the work force, management may enjoy a boost in worker morale. In turn, the outside employer of a specialized crew of cleaners can operate more efficiently. The employee who works for a "maintenance corporation" is often provided with a uniform bearing the company's name, and this and other forms of recognition help to reduce some of the unattractiveness of the job. Moreover (and this is offered as a hypothesis to be tested), the wage and fringe benefits of the specialized (external) maintenance worker are likely to be significantly greater than those received by the lowest-rung worker in a multilevel-skill company hierarchy.

A fourth reason for the use of external services is the periodic need for specialized personnel that many small and medium-sized firms cannot afford to employ on a full-time basis. An illustration of such a situation is the following:

A very small company cannot afford to employ counsel that is competent in very many fields of law. It therefore seems that a small company should not attempt to have any lawyers on its staff but should depend entirely on outside counsel. As a company grows larger, it may develop enough problems in some specific field to justify retaining full-time counsel inside its organization. Therefore, except for the very small and the very large companies there should be some balancing of inside and outside counsel.[3]

The survey by the National Industrial Conference Board cited in footnote 3 showed how specialization operates to increase the use of external services, by pointing up that the use of outside counsel occurred frequently in antitrust, tax, and securities situations in practice before administrative bodies such as the Federal Trade and the Securities and Exchange Commissions, and in areas where litigation is involved.

In an earlier study the Conference Board reported, with respect to another specialized service, insurance, that "few com-

[3] Statement by a vice president of a machinery company in NICB, *Conference Board Business Management Record*, October, 1959: *Organization for Legal Work.*

panies attempt to handle their insurance affairs without advice and assistance from insurance brokers, agents, or other outside consultants." [4]

In the case of the large retail department store mentioned above, management explained that most of the external services are used because the store is not large enough to warrant employing specialized personnel such as lawyers, real estate brokers, public relations experts, sign maintenance workers, architects, engineers, and physicians.

A fifth source of demand for external services arises from the need of companies to adjust to erratic labor requirements. (The difference between this point and the one preceding is that we are now not discussing personnel with highly specialized types of skills.) Firms that experience peak work loads from time to time find it more convenient as well as more economical (less bookkeeping, no fringe benefits, etc.) to hire temporary personnel. The latter are also used to fill in for workers on vacation. The rapid growth of all types of agencies specializing in temporary help underscores the gains to companies using these external services.

In the retail store which we studied, management pointed out that even though the firm has its own data processing department for routine work, it is compelled to use an external service when it has special loads or when the time factor is critical.

The government unit mentioned above also pointed to the seasonal nature of most construction and road maintenance work as a reason for hiring outside firms during the peak months.

A sixth motive for using external services is the desire on the part of many firms to maintain a small, compact, relatively homogeneous labor force.

It is difficult to assess whether or not this is a quantitatively

[4] NICB, *Studies in Business Policy,* No. 81: *Company Insurance Administration.*

significant factor. This type of behavior is found where employment discrimination on the basis of race, creed, color, sex, or age is practiced. If the performance of an essential function requires the hiring of workers whom the firm considers to have undesirable attributes, it may seek recourse instead to external services. While the force operating here resembles that under point three above, namely, the avoidance of troublesome functions, it differs in that it is focused primarily on the type of worker performing the function rather than on the function itself.

Another reason that can be identified as contributory to the increased use of external services is management's desire to enhance the firm's image by being in the forefront of technological or organizational innovations.

It should come as no surprise that many firms purchase external services such as those of management consultants or systems analysts in order to make the statement that they have done so—quite apart from any substantive benefits that may accrue to them. This preoccupation with the corporate image stems in part from the basic structural change in enterprise, analyzed by Berle and Means, namely the divorce of ownership and control.[5] Managers of corporate enterprises find it desirable, or even necessary, to underscore that they possess a high degree of expertise. The management of every firm usually wishes to make a good impression on its stockholders, customers, and workers as well as on the community at large.

Closely allied to the above is the need to imitate competitors. This objective is reinforced by changing market structures. In cases where nonprice competition is prevalent, the emphasis shifts to competition in other areas. This latter type of activity leads to the increased use of such external services as public relations firms, advertising agencies, decorators, pro-

[5] A. A. Berle, Jr. and Gardiner Means, *The Modern Corporation and Private Property, passim.*

fessional writers, and producers of financial reports and sales brochures.

Another identifiable motive for using external services is the necessity to cope with risk and uncertainty, especially in matters of technological change and obsolescence.

This goal can be realized to a greater or less degree by resort to expert advice in matters of finance and insurance. Examples here would involve reliance on services of insurance brokers or industrial engineering consultants, and on leasing instead of outright purchase of plant and equipment.

The leasing example is at once interesting and vexing. It is vexing since, in the strict sense, a firm contracts for the use of a piece of equipment or of a building rather than for a person. Hence, classification of such activity as a producer service is open to question. But it is interesting, since the decision to lease involves many of the considerations discussed in the internal versus external dichotomy. A balanced view of the problem is found in a National Industrial Conference Board survey, which, after noting that certain types of leasing were on the increase (e.g., expensive office equipment, automobiles, and trucks) found that other types were decreasing (e.g., office buildings, warehouses, and tankers). It concluded that:

In the past five years, many companies have changed their opinion about the rationale for leasing. It was once popular to cite the conservation of working capital as a major benefit; very few companies now do so and many regard leasing as an expensive form of borrowing. But experience has demonstrated that leasing rather than buying certain types of equipment brings the company certain operating advantages, such as specialized services from lessors and avoidance of the risk of obsolscence.[6]

Clearly, then, the services aspect of leasing is dominant, and if one were to examine the internal operations of leasing com-

[6] NICB, *Conference Board Business Management Record*, November 1, 1963; *Another Look at Leasing*, p. 47.

panies, one would undoubtedly find that they bear a closer resemblance to financing or factoring than to goods producing firms.

Finally, external services are often called upon to provide guidance with respect to the firm's growth. In pursuit of this objective, firms may utilize the services of economic and financial consultants, management consulting firms, market research firms, investment counselors, and other types of firms specializing in long-range planning.

Factors Contributing to the Growth of Producer Services

The major thrust of the foregoing discussion has been directed to those factors which motivate firms in all sectors of the economy to use external rather than internal resources for the performance of certain service functions. In addition to the possibility of greater shifting or contracting-out of work to external firms on the part of existing firms, there are also certain factors affecting the aggregate levels of producer services that are embedded in the process of economic growth. Such factors as the number of firms in operation, their distribution according to size, the number of new plants and office buildings constructed, government expenditures, changes in technology, trends in the financing of research and development, increasing urbanization, all affect the level of producer services. While many of these factors contribute to the expansion of such services, others may operate to decrease them. For instance, a new architectural trend toward windowless buildings could eliminate the need for window washers. What evidence we have, though, points to a rapidly growing producer services segment.

Chandler and Sayles are of the opinion that the industrial firm is moving in the direction of increased use of outsiders to do specialized work such as construction and maintenance. "We are in business to make our product, not to wash windows," was a typical management comment.[7] The cheif executive of the department store studied remarked, "The major function of this firm is rapid turnover of a highly competitive item [apparel] and functions that are peripheral to this central one are better left to specialists."

The foregoing represents a first effort at identifying the forces influencing the demand for producer services. What the case material and the theoretical analyses suggest is that on balance—largely as a result of potential economies reflecting increased specialization and scale of operations—powerful forces are operating to expand the contracting out of producer services. But we also identified certain trends operating in the opposite direction. A further probing of these and related factors will be attempted in Chapter VII, where the interconnections between economic growth and the expansion of producer services are viewed in larger perspective.

[7] Chandler and Sayles, p. 11.

Chapter IV

THE SUPPLY OF PRODUCER SERVICES

We have alluded to the dearth of detailed data concerning the firms which supply services to other firms, to governments, and to nonprofit organizations. The lack of information about the services sector is partly due, as Stigler observed, to "the smallness of the employing unit, the difficulty of defining output, the greater social concern with employment and output in manufacturing, and the ubiquity of the service industries." [1]

The substantial growth of the services sector of the economy, and of producer services in particular, has proceeded much more rapidly than the elaboration of the conceptual framework and the statistical information required to appraise this transformation. Not even the "computer revolution," with its greatly expanded capacity to provide large bodies of data inexpensively, has as yet closed the gap between the changes under way and our understanding of them.

In the present chapter we will analyze Census and other data which bear on producer services in the aggregate, present the findings of our field interviews with executives in two widely different types of business services (i.e., maintenance and management consulting), and examine the reports and statistics of several publicly held firms in this area.

In Tables 7 and 8, Internal Revenue Service data are presented to show the number of businesses and total business receipts during the year 1961–1962. The categories contained in these two tables differ from those in Tables 1, 2, 4, and 5.

[1] George J. Stigler, *Trends in Output and Employment*, p. 38.

Table 7

SELECTED PRODUCER SERVICES BY TYPE OF ORGANIZATION AND RECEIPTS, 1961–1962

Industry	Number of Businesses				Receipts (millions of dollars)				Average Receipts (thousands of dollars)
	Sole Proprietorships	Partnerships	Corporations	Total	Sole Proprietorships	Partnerships	Corporations	Total	
Transportation, communications, and sanitary services	286,672	18,100	49,048	353,820	4,100	1,167	68,154	73,421	207.5
Wholesale trade	328,130	41,950	123,412	493,492	16,973	12,843	132,514	162,330	328.9
Finance, insurance, and real estate	461,649	207,678	340,210	1,009,537	5,275	4,902	75,584	85,761	11.8
Advertising	18,061	1,557	6,394	26,032	368	124	3,623	4,115	158.1
Services to buildings	28,878	1,897	*	30,775	188	57	*	245	79.6
Other business services	171,364	15,974	32,306	219,644	1,532	667	5,113	7,312	33.3
Legal	124,164	22,071	*	146,235	1,807	2,132	*	3,940	26.9
Engineering and architectural	49,739	5,985	*	55,724	798	753	*	1,551	27.8
Accounting, auditing, and bookkeeping	96,180	9,115	*	105,295	603	926	*	1,529	14.5
Other services	77,158	1,299	17,945	96,402	421	45	3,051	3,511	36.5
All industries	9,241,755	938,966	1,190,286	11,371,007	170,891	73,413	873,178	1,117,572	98.3

* Not applicable.

Source: U.S. Department of the Treasury, Internal Revenue Service, *Statistics of Income, 1961–1962, U.S. Business Tax Returns.*

This is a reflection of the fact that each develops information from a different source, for different purposes.

As Table 7 indicates, the largest number of firms among the producer service industries in 1961–1962 was found in the finance, insurance, and real estate area—over one million businesses, or about 9 percent of all business enterprises in the country. This was followed by wholesale trade, the transportation group, and a miscellaneous category, "other business services." In terms of receipts, however, wholesale trade ranked first, indicating perhaps that while less numerous, the firms here are generally larger than those in the finance group. It is also interesting to note that the latter group exceeded all of the other groups in each type of business structure in number of businesses, but that the absolute number of partnerships was particularly high—a greater number, in fact, than in all of the other groups combined and representing about 22 percent of all partnerships in the country.

Firms in the producer services segment tend to be organized chiefly in sole proprietorships, just as firms in the entire economy and in the services sector are. As Table 8 shows, in all but one of the producer services industries, two-thirds or more of the firms are sole proprietorships. Only in finance, insurance, and real estate was the proportion less than half (45.7 percent). In half of the producer services groups, over 80 percent of the firms were sole proprietorships. The proportion was particularly high in services to dwellings, and in accounting, engineering, and architectural services.

In finance, insurance, and real estate, partnerships constitute over 20 percent of the firms—a higher proportion than in any other business category in the table. Firms providing legal services ranked second among all industries in the proportion of partnerships, but although partnerships constituted only 15 percent of all legal firms, they accounted for 54 percent of the

Table 8
PERCENTAGE DISTRIBUTION OF PRODUCER SERVICES BY TYPE OF ORGANIZATION AND RECEIPTS, 1961–1962

Industry	Firms				Receipts			
	Sole Proprietorships	Partnerships	Corporations	Total	Sole Proprietorships	Partnerships	Corporations	Total
Transportation, communications, water supply, electric, gas, and sanitary services	81.0	5.1	13.9	100.0	5.6	1.6	92.8	100.0
Wholesale trade	66.5	8.5	25.0	100.0	10.5	7.9	81.6	100.0
Finance, insurance, and real estate	45.7	20.6	33.7	100.0	6.2	5.7	88.1	100.0
Advertising	69.4	6.0	24.6	100.0	8.9	3.0	88.0	100.0
Services to dwellings	93.8	6.2	*	100.0	76.7	23.3	*	100.0
Other business services	78.0	7.3	14.7	100.0	21.0	9.1	69.9	100.0
Legal	84.9	15.1	*	100.0	45.9	54.1	*	100.0
Engineering and architectural	89.3	10.7	*	100.0	51.5	48.5	*	100.0
Accounting, auditing, and bookkeeping	91.3	8.7	*	100.0	39.4	60.6		100.0
All industries	81.3	8.3	10.5	100.0	15.3	6.6	78.1	100.0

* Not applicable.
Source: Same as for Table 7.

receipts, indicating that they are the larger and more important firms in that business category.

Corporations are more numerous than partnerships, but not more numerous than sole ownerships, in the five industries where the corporate form exists. One-third of the firms in finance and one-fourth of the firms in wholesale trade are corporations, with smaller proportions in transportation and other producer services.

From 1945–1946 to 1961–1962, as Table 9 indicates, firms in the producer services industries did not show any great change with respect to the form of business organization. The corporate form increased slightly in transportation, wholesale trade, and in all industries, while in both transportation and all industries individual proprietorships and partnerships declined. However, there was an increase in the single proprietorship ratios in finance from 35.9 to 45.7 percent and in the partnership ratios from 19.2 to 20.6 percent. The role of the corporation in this field, at least in terms of the number of firms, dropped from 44.9 to 33.7 percent of the total; however, in receipts, corporate enterprise participation rose from 81.8 to 88.1 percent.

The general picture that emerges in finance, then, is that relatively more individuals entered the field during the postwar period, probably engaging in the small brokerage business and selling over-the-counter securities, insurance, and mutual funds. It may be noted parenthetically that no minimum cash balance was required at that time for membership in the National Association of Securities Dealers.

In terms of business receipts, corporations are more important than any other enterprise form in those industries where corporations are to be found. The range is from 92.8 percent of all receipts in transportation accruing to corporations, to roughly 78 percent in other producer services. Sole proprietorships received most of the receipts in the services-to-dwellings

Table 9

CHANGES IN SELECTED PRODUCER SERVICES BY TYPE OF ORGANIZATION
AND RECEIPTS, 1945 AND 1961

Percentage of Businesses

Industry	Sole Proprietorship		Partnership		Corporation	
	1945–46	*1961–62*	*1945–46*	*1961–62*	*1945–46*	*1961–62*
Transportation, com- munications, etc.	82.1	81.0	6.1	5.1	11.8	13.9
Wholesale trade	60.8	66.5	15.6	8.5	23.6	25.0
Finance, insurance, and real estate	35.9	45.7	19.2	20.6	44.9	33.7
All industries	82.8	81.3	9.1	8.3	8.0	10.5

Percentage of Receipts

Industry	Sole Proprietorship		Partnership		Corporation	
	1945–46	*1961–62*	*1945–46*	*1961–62*	*1945–46*	*1961–62*
Transportation, com- munications, etc.	5.1	5.6	2.1	1.6	92.9	92.8
Wholesale trade	12.3	10.5	14.2	7.9	73.5	81.6
Finance, insurance, and real estate	7.1	6.2	11.0	5.7	81.8	88.1
All industries	16.0	15.3	9.6	6.6	74.4	78.1

Source: Same as for Table 7.

category. In the area of legal services and in engineering and architectural services, sole proprietorships and partnerships shared receipts almost equally. Some changes are noticeable in receipts during the post-World War II years, when the share of corporate receipts in wholesale trade increased from 73.5 percent in 1945 to 81.6 percent in 1961; advertising corporations likewise show a considerable rise—from 66.1 percent in the earlier year to 88 percent in 1961. Average annual receipts per firm have increased: in transportation from $125,000 to $200,000, and in wholesale trade from $249,000 to $325,000. Advertising showed a rise from $77,100 in 1945 to $156,500 in 1961. Other increases posted were: legal services, from $10,500 to $26,900; accounting, from $11,400 to $14,500; and engineering, from $13,600 to $27,800.[2]

It is interesting to speculate on the relationships between the legal form of enterprises and their function. Referring to Table 8 and using the "all industries" distribution as a norm, we may note that the transportation group does not differ materially from the basic pattern. The wholesale trade category, on the other hand, shows some significant deviations. There are fewer sole proprietorships and more corporations than in all industries, owing in part to the need for large amounts of capital and the economies of scale that can be realized from, for instance, larger warehouses. Very significant differences exist with respect to the finance, insurance, and real estate area. Sole proprietorships are about one-half as frequent as in the all industries group, whereas partnerships and corporations are roughly three times as prevalent. Partial explanations for this are the need for larger amounts of capital, particularly in banking and insurance, along with the need for maintaining close personal relationships and projecting an image of responsibility—prerequisites in the investment banking and securities fields. In recent years there has been a noticeable tendency among secu-

[2] Stigler, *Trends in Employment in the Service Industries*, Table 14, p. 56; and U.S. Department of the Treasury, *Statistics of Income, 1961–62*.

rities firms to change from partnerships to corporations. In advertising, the pattern is one of the relatively greater importance of large firms, probably due less to the possible realization of economies of scale—though they may be considerable—than to the fact that the buyer is itself usually a firm.

The high proportion of sole proprietorships in the services-to-dwellings industry is to be expected, since individuals can fairly easily clean windows, wax floors, and do other maintenance jobs with very little capital investment. These are highly labor intensive activities. The absence from the foregoing tables of data for corporations in this area is probably due to definitional problems, since there are some very large corporations active in this field, one of which, in fact, receives detailed treatment in the present chapter.

In the area of legal services, strong taboos exist with respect to incorporation, on the theory that the personal responsibility of the attorney to his client would be diluted thereby. Hence, the absence of an entry under corporations is undoubtedly correct, although some court jurisdictions have recently begun to permit the incorporation of legal firms. The same explanation holds in large part for the engineering and architectural as well as the accounting and auditing fields.

Producer services firms tend to be located in close proximity to their customers, which in many instances are manufacturing concerns who find it necessary or expedient to buy from others rather than to perform certain services for themselves. The other major factor influencing the location of producer services firms is the heavy concentration of diversified enterprises in large urban centers. (These and other locational aspects are treated in greater detail in Chapter VI.)

Technological change is also important; for example, certain services such as electronic data processing can now be performed long distance via coaxial cable or wireless transmission. It is not necessary, therefore, for data processing bureaus to be

located near their customers. By way of contrast, certain services such as building and office maintenance must be performed at set locations, and there appear to be no technological changes on the horizon which can alter this.

What, if anything, can be said about productivity trends
in producer services? Most economists would tend to agree
with the following summary: Productivity has been generally
higher in the goods than in the services sector; yet transportation and communications, both of which have very large producer services components have shown the most rapid gains in
factor productivity during the past half century; difficult as it
is to derive valid measures of productivity in the goods sector,
the problems are much more complex in the services sector. In
finance and insurance for instance, most of the estimates are
imputed, since the services are not sold directly. In point of
fact, Gary S. Becker [3] maintains that downward biases exist in
current measures of productivity in the services area, due in
large part to the exclusion of a monetary value of the time
spent by households in acquiring certain services. The major
research project on productivity in the services sector of the
economy now being carried on by the National Bureau of Economic Research, which Victor Fuchs is directing, will it is
hoped, reduce the substantial amount of uncertainty that pre-
vails in this relatively neglected area.

We are not in a position to contribute to this task directly,
although it is our considered judgment that wherever producer
services are able to utilize large amounts of capital, and the
rate of technological change is rapid, there is no reason why
these industries should not show an above average gain in productivity. Those producer services which can avail themselves
to a high degree of the revolutionary developments in compu-
terization—data processing firms, for example—are prime can-
didates for such a demonstration.

[3] Gary S. Becker, "A Theory of the Allocation of Time," *Economic Journal*,
LXXV (September, 1965), 507.

Much more complex and subtle is the situation where the key resource is personnel rather than capital, but where the quality of the personnel is undergoing marked improvement. There is no reason why certain producer services of a technical type, such as market research, should not experience quite rapid gains in productivity as a result of a substantial increase in the educational level of their staffs. Yet, here the measurement question—as in many other areas of the services sector—poses formidable problems which can only be resolved by much more comprehensive and intensive studies.

One of the most interesting aspects of this problem is the fact that firms in the producer services segment contribute directly as well as indirectly to productivity gains in other areas of the economy. (This indeed is one of their basic *raisons d' être.*) Of course, reverse influences are also at work, thus compounding the difficulties of isolating specific effects.

Maintenance and Consulting: Two Extremes
in the Producer Services Spectrum

In order to attain a deeper insight into the producer services segment, we undertook field work in two widely disparate types of producer services, namely, maintenance and management consulting. They are polar types for two reasons: the educational levels of their work forces, and their basic economic functions. In the maintenance case under review, less than one percent were college graduates, whereas in the consulting firms, the ratio of college graduates to total employed approached 80 percent. With respect to the economic functions, plant maintenance is essentially a routine current activity, whereas management consulting should be viewed as an element in the investment process bearing high order significance for the long-run direction and growth of the firm. What they have in common, of course, is that they are both producer services; the former is an example of what we have termed perishable producer services, and the latter of durable producer services. Additional light on the dynamics of the producer services segment was gained from studying the operations and becoming acquainted with the orientation of the managements.

A Supplier of Maintenance Services. Although perishable producer services traditionally have a low-status function, the maintenance of factories, private and public buildings, and stadia is currently a multimillion-dollar industry and is growing. One estimate put the number of firms engaged in contract maintenance in the U.S. at about 4,500 with total annual revenues expected to exceed 505 million dollars by the end of 1965, a 29 percent increase over the previous year.[4] More than 70 percent of all buildings put up after 1945 in the City of New York are cleaned under contracts, that is to say, by external cleaning or maintenance firms.

The many-sided aspects of the business of providing external maintenance are well illustrated by one of the country's largest maintenance firms. The background of this company is of some interest. Based in the City of New York, it is more than 75 years old and currently employs about 13,000 workers. Its gross billings in 1964 were $58 million, with a net income of just over $1 million, and future billings are expected to rise.

The major types of services provided by this firm are maintenance and cleaning operations at office buildings, railroad stations, department stores, sports stadia, airports, shopping centers, major expositions, and fairs. In some cases, related services such as watchmen, policemen, doormen, and porters are also provided. Other major segments of this firm's operations include aircraft fueling, aircraft and engine maintenance, atomic and chemical waste disposal, and equipment leasing.

[4] The New York *Times,* February 17, 1965.

The diversity of operations is obviously very great, yet they can all be subsumed under the producer services portmanteau. The firm was privately held until 1959, when it made its first public offering of stock. Since that time several mergers and acquisitions were consummated, which accounted in part for the growth in total billings.

The firm's relations with its labor force appears to be somewhat atypical when compared with firms in some other service industries, but since this aspect is at the heart of the firm's operations, some additional comment is warranted. In his work on the service industries, Stigler [5] indicated that building service and maintenance workers fell in a unionization range of 20 to 40 percent; in the firm under review, 100 percent of the workers are covered by union contracts. The immense labor relations problem is evident from the fact that 35 different unions, with 110 separate contracts, are involved. Approximately 1½ contracts are negotiated each week! Many employers, seeing to avoid dealing with multiple unions, contract out for maintenance. This is one of the firm's principal "selling points."

Since routine maintenance typically requires little skill, and since the firm is located in New York, it is not surprising to find that the work force is composed mainly of members of minority groups who have lacked the opportunity to acquire extensive, formal educational training and higher occupational skills. The firm's work force is composed of Eastern Europeans, Puerto Ricans, Cubans, and Negroes. About 85 percent of the employees who are presently in their twenties have had some high school education, while few in the 35 and over age group have had any.

The turnover rate, which was once much higher, has now been reduced to about 32 percent per year. Minimum hourly wage rates range from $1.87 in Brooklyn to $2.02 in Manhat-

[5] Stigler, *Trends in Employment in the Service Industries*, p. 58.

tan. Porters' rates range from $2.30 to $2.42. On the upper end of the wage scale, airport fueling operators and truckers earn from $9,000 to $12,000 annually.

A dramatic example of this firm's ability to assemble and supervise a large work force in a short period of time is the World's Fair maintenance operation. In August of 1963, for instance, some 70 workers were involved; this number grew to 200 by March of 1964 and to 4,000 by May of 1964. At peak, it reached 5,000 in May of 1965. The logistics involved in interviewing, processing, training, supervising, and payroll dispensing can be compared only to that of a military operation. One of the interesting aspects that came to light during this hiring process was the existence of a large pool of workers willing to accept a purely temporary position. The company has had to rely less on college students than it thought would be the case. Undoubtedly, both the company and the temporary workers will benefit from the association. The former will have a greater pool of workers with some needed skills and the latter will have acquired some skills and knowledge of the company's operations that may develop into more permanent jobs.

As was mentioned earlier, this firm also has an atomic waste disposal operation. In this activity it must deal with employees of above average scientific and technical skill. Entry into this relatively new and highly technical area was gained by purchasing one of the two established companies in the field. A physicist, knowledgeable in atomic waste disposal, was hired away from a government unit and placed in charge of technical personnel training. He is assisted by an outside consultant. The necessary unskilled workers (e.g., cleaners and riggers) are drawn from the firm's general labor force on a voluntary basis. Incidentally, the ability to draw on a large pool of relatively unskilled labor is of special importance in this field, since by frequent rotation each worker's exposure to radiation is reduced to a minimum. Supervisors are all professionals with either a Bachelor's or a Master's degree,

A discussion with the president on the precise function of the firm in the production process brought out the fact that he conceived of the company's role not as one of creating new jobs but merely of performing jobs transferred from an internal to an external function. He characterized most businessmen as "lazy" in their reluctance to transfer their managerial talents from the production function proper to the service areas of their operations. Hence, he maintained, his firm "lives off the inefficiencies of business concerns."

The firm believes that one of the important areas of potential growth is the provision of services to groups of firms on a cooperative basis, at reduced costs through economies of scale. One example is a proposal for a "supermarket" of replacement parts for all airlines. The individual airlines would gain in having any and all parts readily available at lower cost because of bulk purchasing. This firm is acutely aware of the existence of many essential service functions which are presently being performed inefficiently and at high cost, and is exploring innovations in the organization and supply of such services to capture the potential market. In this connection, the head of the firm commented that nonprofit organizations such as hospitals and universities are particularly inefficient in service operations. Nevertheless, he is loath to enter these areas since experience has demonstrated that local, political, and other pressures are especially prevalent in them and tend to result in the hiring and protection of substandard inefficient workers at low wages.

One of the major sources of the increased productivity of the external service firm's labor force relative to an internal work force is the quality and quantity of supervision (including the setting and enforcing of predetermined work standards) in the external firm. In this firm, for instance, a typical 25 man cleaning crew would have one supervisor and one or two foremen, a much larger supervisory ratio than is typically found in firms providing their own maintenance. Such a structure is possible only because of scale and specialization.

Specialization in maintance has led to technological changes in the form of the introduction of lighter and more efficient cleaning equipment and such changes, in turn, accelerate specialization. For example, windows are now cleaned with screwless squeegees made of aluminum, whereas they were formerly made of brass and required the unfastening and fastening of about a dozen screws in order to change the rubber wiper. Other innovations have been electric scrubbing and waxing machines, improved detergents, and in recent years the use of electric power scaffolds in the cleaning of office building windows. It is reasonable to suppose that the external specialized firm is in a better position than an internal maintenance crew to become aware of, assess, develop, and actually use the most modern equipment. In this way, a relatively permanent margin of efficiency over internal maintenance workers can be realized.

In the discussion of the effect of business fluctuations on the firm, it was indicated that the firm's billings are relatively inelastic with respect to business downturns. The rationale is that since there is a cost saving in contracting out, "pulling the work back in," would swiftly lead to a deterioration in the level of service, with perhaps little decrease in expenditure. Even when stores are on their way to bankruptcy, it was alleged, they tend to "stick with the firm to the end." Good maintenance is a basic factor in continuing operations. This raises the general question of the elasticity of demand for services on the part of firms, and suggests that the demand at least for some perishable types may be more inelastic than would appear at first sight.

Our review of the development and operations of one large maintenance firm has called attention to a range of factors that initially contributed to the growth of this type of specialized producer services, and that continued to contribute to its growth. The key factors appear to be the increased opportuni-

ties for specialization incident to the growth of the economy at
large, with gains in efficiency centered largely on the more
effective recruitment, training, and supervision of the work
force.

Suppliers of Consulting Services. No enterprise stands in
sharper contrast to a maintenance firm than a business consulting organization, whose major service relates less to current
operations than to the long-run growth and profitability of the
clients' enterprises. These consulting firms are interesting in
their own right, and a study of them, by affording a point of
contrast to the maintenance firm, may also contribute to a
deeper understanding of producer services in general.

There are only two major sources of data on management
consulting firms; one is the *Census of Business* and the other a
trade group, the Association of Consulting Management Engineers, Inc. (ACME) in the City of New York. Under the heading "Business, management consulting services," the *Census of
Business, 1963,* listed a total of 20,879 establishments. Of these,
7,793 had a payroll. The total receipts of all consulting establishments were $1,206 million, with 92 percent of the receipts
going to those units with payrolls. Other data that could be
derived from these sources are that average receipts per establishment amounted to $57,799; average wages per employee to
$6,175. Data from ACME, however, list a total of only 2,200
firms in 1958 and 2,500 in 1962, with billings in the latter year
of 650 million dollars.[6] A smaller difference appears with respect to total billings. Census data indicate 653 million dollars
in 1958 and 1.2 billion dollars in 1963, and ACME reports 650
million dollars in 1962.

Apart from possible differences between the Census Bureau

[6] Data interpolated from mimeographed chart, *Growth of Management Consulting Firms in North America, 1910–1962,* prepared by Association of Consulting Management Engineers. (I am indebted to Mr. Philip Shay, Secretary
of ACME, for many of the estimates cited herein.)

and ACME regarding the definition of consulting services per se, an obvious discrepancy in the number of firms arises from the fact that Census data are reported on an establishment or branch basis, whereas ACME's data refer to the firms. Obviously, many firms operate more than one branch.

Table 10 shows how much more rapidly consulting firms

Table 10

ALL FIRMS AND CONSULTING FIRMS IN THE
UNITED STATES, 1910 TO 1962 [a]

Year	Total Number of Firms	Percent Change from Previous Decade	Number of Consulting Firms	Percent Change from Previous Decade
1910	1,515,000	n.a.	15	n.a.
1920	1,821,000	20.2	30	100.0
1930	2,993,700	6.4	200	567.0
1940	3,291,000	1.0	400	100.0
1950	4,051,000	23.1	1,500	275.0
1960	4,658,000	15.0	2,400	60.0
1962	4,755,000	n.a.	2,500	n.a.

N.a.: not available.

[a] Excludes agricultural and some professional service firms.

Sources: U.S. Department of Commerce, Bureau of the Census, *Historical Statistics of the United States, Colonial Times to 1957,* and *Statistical Abstract of the United States;* and data on consulting firms from Association of Consulting Management Engineers, Inc.

have grown than all firms between 1910 to 1962. The lower absolute numbers of consulting firms account for the vastly larger percentage changes shown, but their growth is nonetheless impressive. Fifteen consulting firms with half a million dollars in billings grew to some 2,500 firms with billings exceeding 650 million dollars over this period. In the past two decades alone, all firms increased by some 47.6 percent, but consulting firms grew by 500 percent—more than ten times as fast. This extraordinary growth pattern, however, should be tempered by the finding of a slower current rate of growth, which is estimated by ACME to be about 4 percent per annum.

An index of the coming of age of the consulting business is provided by ACME's estimate that 70 to 75 percent of the larger firms in our economy employ outside consultants. Lawrence A. Appley, president of the American Management Association, gives further evidence of the importance of the management function (both internal and external) in the statement, "The number of managers enrolled in formal management training programs within their own companies, in universities and colleges, with management consultants or in professional societies has grown from less than 10,000 a year in 1948 to over 600,000 in 1962.[7]

A greater depth of understanding of the data was made possible through interviews with three prominent management consulting firms.

Case one is among the oldest and largest consulting firms in the country, having been founded in 1914. The current work force numbers 700, of which 450, or 64.7 percent, are professional personnel, including 280 with advanced degrees. Since its inception this firm has completed about 40,000 assignments for 4,000 clients. In a recent year, the firm completed 1,500 assignments for 800 clients. The approach of this firm to the consulting field is one of concentrating on the key problems that determine the growth, success, and profitability of an enterprise. These problems include productivity, cost reduction, management appraisal, long- and short-run economic studies, and similar investigations. Most of the clients are large businesses, but there appears to be a growing use of the firm's services by nonprofit and government units.

A sampling of the problems currently worked on includes design and development of special products, cost reduction, productivity improvement, management controls, systems development, computer installations, and reliability analysis.

A principal of this firm indicated his belief that the branch of

[7] Lawrence A. Appley, "Manager Training in Proper Perspective," in *AMA, A Description* (brochure).

the consulting field growing most rapidly is that composed of firms offering specialized services such as site selection, paperwork handling, and numbering systems. The National Records Management Council estimates, for example, that the number of specialists in the field of systematic records management and disposal has more than doubled in the past decade.[8]

The main element in the success of consulting companies, it was stressed, is high quality personnel. This firm estimated that gross billings of the industry are growing at the rate of about two to two and a half times that of the Gross National Product.

Case two is another of the country's large consulting firms. The total billings currently are at a rate of about 23 million dollars annually. The staff numbers around 725, of whom 570, about 80 percent, are professionals. The five major divisions of the firm are management services, life sciences, research and development, engineering, and equipment manufacturing. The last function is an unusual one for consulting firms. It was indicated that the management services division has grown the fastest during the past decade. This firm experienced its most rapid expansion between 1945 and 1960, when it grew at the rate of 15 percent annually. Since 1963 the company has been relatively stable.

A senior member of the firm stated that there are few economies of scale in the consulting field, so that there is no incentive for continuous growth. He emphasized that since a consulting firm works on a wide variety of problems, and since its personnel have widely differing backgrounds, it is most important that the staff know each other and learn to communicate informally on a continuing basis. A rapid increase in personnel tends to retard this.

Not only is there a strong current demand for consulting services, but, as one executive stated, good consulting firms

[8] The *Wall Street Journal*, February 23, 1965.

create their own demand by finding new services to perform for clients. Contrary to the representations of most popular writing in this field, his firm seldom if ever acts as a "company doctor" coming to the rescue of companies in trouble. Rather, the consulting firm seeks the "identification and exploitation of growth opportunities" for its clients.

A discussion of the role of government as a user of management service elicited the response that the government market is an expanding, albeit a volatile, one. Currently, however, 35 to 40 percent of this firm's work is for different levels of government—a rather high figure. The major reason given by this firm for the growth of consulting services in general is the secular increase in capital investment per employee and the consequent need for close attention to long-range planning and for staying abreast of technological change.

Case three is also one of the larger management consulting firms. Total staff numbers about 460, about equally divided between professional consulting staff and supporting personnel. Virtually 100 percent of the professional staff and 65 percent of the total staff are college graduates. In the last ten years the professional staff increased 2½ times—from 90 to 230. One of the significant growth segments of this firm is its international business, with currently 20 percent of the staff working outside the U.S.

An indication of the strong and persistent demand for this firm's services is revealed by the statement that there has not been a reduction in staff in the past 35 years. It was stated, also, that during the past 15 years there has never been a problem of underutilization. In fact, the problem is more often the reverse—there are frequent periods when the work load is excessive.

The firm's professional staff is recruited in part from business school graduates in their middle or late twenties with little or no prior experience, and partly from those in the 28 to 34 year old age group who have had graduate training as well as some business experience. Unlike cases one and two above, this firm does little government and nonprofit work. As in cases one and two above, it has very few clients with fewer than 500 employees.

It is worth noting that several senior members in the firm stated that cost reduction *per se* is not the dominant reason for their being retained, nor is it their major talking point. The primary concern of the firm is with the organizational problems of the client, especially as they relate to defining and clarifying objectives. A sizable amount of this firm's current work has to do with merger and acquisition problems. Immediate profit improvement, it was stressed, is not the test of the firm's services. Rather, it is the acceptance and implementation by the client of the firm's recommendations that are the important desiderata.

Another interesting statement emphasized that although each consulting job has is unique features, there is a great deal of technical carry-over from one job to the next that has enabled this firm (as well as other consulting firms) to build a body of techniques or "social inventions" that have broad applicability.

Emphasizing the strong demand for the firm's services, the officials stated that since World War II each year's billings have exceeded those of the previous year. The current growth of the firm is limited mainly by the ability to attract qualified personnel and to develop competent supervisors—a theme stressed in each of the cases studied.

The image that these particular firms have of themselves conforms very well to Arthur H. Cole's description:

At their very best, outside consultants and researchers really do more than help solve business problems, even though that activity is important in itself. The consultants and researchers also play vital

Table 11

FINANCIAL AND EMPLOYMENT DATA, SELECTED PUBLICLY HELD PRODUCER SERVICE COMPANIES, 1959 AND 1964

Company	Nature of Service	Gross Billings (millions)			Total Employment			Earnings Per Share (dollars)		
		1959	1964	Percent Change 1959–64	1959	1964	Percent Change 1959–64	1959	1964	Percent Change 1959–64
Allied Maintenance	General maintenance	28.2	58.1	106.0	n.a.	5,040		.66	1.24	87.9
National Cleaning Contractors, Inc.	General maintenance	13.0	29.7	128.5	n.a.	n.a.		.45	1.35	144.4
Foote, Cone and Belding	Advertising	109.6	191.1	74.4	n.a.	1,400		.52	1.09	109.6
Dun and Bradstreet	Publications and services for management	140.5	180.8	28.7	9,576	16,500	72.3	1.49	2.41	61.7
Burns International Detective Agency	Protective services	24.2	43.2	78.5	n.a.	n.a.		.68	1.70	150.0
Kelly Girl Service	Temporary manpower	14.7	37.7	156.5	n.a.	n.a.		.21	1.01	381.0
Manpower, Inc.	Temporary manpower	14.9	37.1	149.0	n.a.	n.a.		.53	1.47	177.4
A. C. Nielsen Co.	Advertising	26.9	45.3	68.4	3,900	5,114	31.1	.63	1.88	198.4
Walter H. Heller Co.	Finance	23.2	45.0	94.0	328	1,555	374.0	.69	.82	18.8

N.a.: not available.
Source: Annual reports of respective companies.

roles in helping to identify and define the problems, in transmitting modern managerial techniques and attitudes, and in acting as catalytic agents to induce change and progress.[9]

Some Publicly Held Producer Services Firms

One of the important pieces of evidence supporting the view that the producer services segment is one of above average growth is the fact that in recent years several large firms have made public offerings of their stock. Table 11 presents selective financial data drawn from their published reports.

While a period of four to five years is certainly insufficient to indicate trends, the performance of most of these firms with respect to gross billings and earnings per share is impressive. Nine out of ten showed percentage gains in gross billings exceeding the percent change in the Gross National Product over the period, and the one exception fell short of the GNP gain by less than 1 percent. In earnings per share, nine out of ten firms exceeded the percentage gain recorded by the firms comprising the Dow Jones Industrials Index, with the one exception falling short by only about 1 percent.[10] As far as employment is concerned, for each of the firms for which data are available, there was a greater percentage increase in employment over this period than in total civilian employment. To some extent, these gains overstate the growth in the sense that some firms expanded at least partly through mergers and acquisitions.

The present chapter has delineated—to the extent permitted by general data and supplemented by case studies—a profile of producer services, with special attention to critical factors influencing their growth. Except for passing references, however, the manpower dimensions involved in their growth was not dealt with. This becomes the subject of the next chapter.

---

[9] Arthur H. Cole, "An Approach to the Study of Entrepreneurship," in Stanley C. Hollander, *Business Consultants and Clients, Michigan State University Business Studies*, p. 1.

[10] Using an annual average of quarterly data on earnings per share of the Dow Jones Industrials average.

Chapter V

THE LABOR FORCE IN THE
PRODUCER SERVICES SEGMENT

The easiest way to gain an overview of the manpower factor in producer services is to begin by assessing the total numbers employed in the major segments and to review the changes in these totals over time. A more refined analysis can then be undertaken, focusing on the types of persons employed, with particular reference to their principal characteristics in terms of sex, race, and earnings.

Occupational Analysis

The usual view of employment in the services sector as a whole is one of relatively high female employment, concentrated in the clerical and personal services and sales occupations, with relatively low pay scales.[1] Our most significant finding is that this picture is misleading for producer services. The latter has a greater percentage of males and higher average earnings than are shown for the labor force as a whole, for the goods sector alone, or for the consumer services segment. Some industries in producer services employ higher than average proportions of professional and managerial personnel, while others are relatively heavy users of craftsmen, operatives, and laborers.

For the reasons adumbrated earlier, we will center attention on the following groups of producer services—those that have not been previously subjected to detailed analysis and which

[1] Stigler, *Trends in Employment in the Service Industries,* p. 58.

are among the more dynamic divisions of the whole producer services segment: advertising; miscellaneous business services; engineering and architectural services; accounting, auditing, and bookkeeping; and miscellaneous professional services. These five industries had a labor force of over a million in 1960. Transportation and wholesale trade, which together had a work force estimated at more than 4 million in 1960, are such large industries relative to the whole segment that it was deemed wise to present occupational distributions which both include and exclude these areas. Also, in order to highlight characteristics that are more or less specific to this segment, the present chapter excludes from the analysis any industry where less than three-fourths of its labor force and/or output were estimated to be devoted to the producer services function. Consequently, the labor force of four industries (i.e., communications, finance, legal services, and government), comprising over 5 million workers as of 1960, has been classified as "other producer services" in the subsequent tables. In addition, we have not made any attempt to present the occupational or other characteristics of the several million persons in the "nonproduction worker" category who provide producer services within firms.

Our occupational analysis is confined then to about 66 percent of the 8.5 million persons we estimate to be engaged directly in external producer services. It was found that no strongly marked occupational pattern can be discerned among the seven industries under analysis. A fairly sharp distinction can be drawn between the occupational distribution in the five business and professional service industries and the producer services aspects of transportation and wholesale trade. However, the dominant size of the latter, despite stationary and declining employment trends, largely determines the occupational ratios for the producer services as a whole.

The occupational distribution of those attached to the business and professional services industries reveals the heavy dependence on professional, technical, and scientific personnel (Table 12). In 1960 these workers constituted 11.2 percent of the employed labor force, 15.9 percent of the employment in all service industries, and 17.3 percent of employment in consumer service industries. But in the same year 36.8 percent of employment in the five business and professional service industries together was in the professional, scientific, and technical category. The range was from about 18 percent in advertising and in miscellaneous business services to 66 to 71 percent in the other three producer services industries. From 1950 to 1960, the proportion of professional personnel in the business and professional services industries dropped slightly, rising in three of the components and falling in two. The professional ratio decrease in the accounting, bookkeeping, and auditing group appears to be the result of a relative increase in clerical personnel—an indication perhaps of further job breakdown and standardization, which make possible more routine processing in bookkeeping and accounting functions. For all other industry categories listed in Table 12, there was a rising trend in the proportion of professionals from 1950 to 1960.

When an overview of the entire producer services segment is sought, including transportation and wholesale trade, the preponderance of professionals disappears. The overall average for the producer services industries is 9.5 percent, a ratio below that for the economy as a whole.

A different picture emerges from an analysis of the managerial classification, which includes many self-employed persons and proprietors. It is not surprising that wholesale trade should have one-fifth of its total employment in the managerial group. A relatively high proportion is also found in advertising, but lower than average ratios in some of the other business and

Table 12

PERCENTAGE DISTRIBUTION BY OCCUPATION OF PERSONS EMPLOYED IN SELECTED PRODUCER SERVICES, 1950 AND 1960

	Profes-sional	Mana-gerial	Clerical	Sales	Crafts-men	Opera-tives	Service Excluding Household	Laborers	All Other	Total
Transportation										
1950	2.0	7.9	15.9	0.4	17.8	36.8	4.1	14.7	0.4	100.0
1960	2.4	8.4	17.2	0.7	16.5	40.1	3.4	10.2	1.1	100.0
Wholesale trade										
1950	2.5	20.5	21.3	20.7	6.0	21.0	1.2	6.6	0.2	100.0
1960	3.0	19.0	22.1	22.7	6.7	18.3	1.0	5.8	1.4	100.0
All producer services										
1950	6.4	12.8	18.8	8.0	12.5	27.7	3.2	10.3	0.3	100.0
1960	9.5	12.5	20.9	9.1	11.2	25.4	3.3	6.8	1.3	100.0
All consumer services										
1950	15.3	13.6	16.9	13.0	7.9	8.0	16.3	2.5	6.5	100.0
1960	17.3	11.3	19.1	11.8	7.3	6.6	17.1	2.4	7.1	100.0
All services										
1950	13.6	13.4	17.2	12.0	8.8	11.9	13.9	4.0	5.3	100.0
1960	15.9	11.5	19.4	11.3	8.0	10.0	14.7	3.2	6.0	100.0
All goods										
1950	3.6	4.0	7.2	1.7	19.5	29.0	1.2	8.2	25.6	100.0
1960	6.2	5.1	9.3	2.5	21.9	30.9	1.2	7.1	15.8	100.0
All goods and services										
1950	8.7	8.8	12.3	7.0	13.8	18.4	7.6	6.0	15.9	100.0
1960	11.2	8.4	14.4	7.2	13.5	19.9	8.4	4.8	13.7	100.0

Advertising										
1950	17.1	21.4	28.7	15.5	9.1	5.8	1.0	0.9	0.5	100.0
1960	17.9	23.7	31.2	12.2	6.7	4.9	0.8	1.1	1.5	100.0
Miscellaneous business services										
1950	16.1	14.5	30.5	3.4	13.0	8.8	12.3	1.1	0.3	100.0
1960	17.5	11.3	31.8	3.9	10.6	8.6	13.3	1.6	1.4	100.0
Engineering and architectural services										
1950	71.2	4.7	15.0	0.7	3.9	3.4	0.3	0.5	0.3	100.0
1960	71.4	4.9	14.0	0.5	4.6	2.9	0.7	0.4	0.6	100.0
Accounting, bookkeeping, and auditing										
1950	71.7	3.0	23.8	0.4	0.3	0.5	0.1	n.a.	0.2	100.0
1960	65.8	2.2	30.4	0.2	0.2	0.1	0.2	n.a.	0.9	100.0
Miscellaneous professional services										
1950	77.3	3.3	10.3	0.5	3.3	2.2	2.5	0.3	0.3	100.0
1960	66.0	4.6	15.7	1.2	5.3	2.6	2.2	0.4	2.0	100.0
All business and professional services										
1950	40.1	11.3	24.6	4.5	7.7	5.4	5.4	0.7	0.3	100.0
1960	36.8	9.8	27.2	3.5	7.4	5.7	7.3	1.0	1.3	100.0

N.a.: not available.
Source: U. S. Department of Commerce, Bureau of the Census, *Census of Population, 1950 and 1960.*

professional industries brings the average for the five industries to the same level as that of the economy, below that of the producer services segment as a whole, and below the total services sector.

Clerical personnel are more heavily represented among producer services as a whole and in several of its components than they are in the entire labor force, the goods sector, and the services sector as a whole. The sales personnel ratio is greater in the producer services segment than it is in the goods sector and in the total labor force. Particularly high proportions of clerical employees are found in advertising, miscellaneous business services, and accounting. Sales personnel were especially prominent in wholesale trade and advertising.

Since the white collar occupations predominate, it will come as no surprise that the remaining occupational categories—craftsmen, operatives, service workers, laborers—are underrepresented among the five business and professional services industries. The producer services industries as a whole have an average proportion of the blue collar occupations.

From Table 12 one finds that compared with consumer services, producer services industries employ relatively fewer professionals, sales, service workers, and laborers; relatively more operatives and craftsmen; and about the same proportion of managers and clerical workers. The trends in producer and consumer services were much the same in 1950 as in 1960. In both groups, the percentage of professionals and clericals increased, and the percentage of managers, craftsmen, operatives, and laborers decreased, from 1950 to 1960. Producer services showed a slight increase in the proportion of sales workers, while this group declined slightly among the consumer services. Likewise, service workers (except private household) rose in relative importance from 1950 to 1960 among consumer services, but remained almost the same in producer services.

Male/Female Ratios

We can acquire a better perspective of the special characteristics of producer services by examining the occupational structure separately for males and females, as shown in Tables 13a
and 13b. It becomes clear that the exceptionally high ratios of
professionals in the business and professional service industries
are primarily due to the presence of the male workers. In every
one of the five such industries, male professionals were heavily
overrepresented, in comparison with the total labor force, but
only in two, miscellaneous professional services and accounting, were females overrepresented in 1960. It is also note-
worthy that the proportion of female professionals in the five
industries fell rather sharply from 1950 to 1960, from 20.2 percent to 14.5 percent of total female employment. The proportion of professionals among both males and females in transportation and wholesale trade was very low. It appears that
male professionals in all producer services combined occurred
in just about the same proportion as they did among the total
employed; male professionals in the producer services were,
however, relatively less numerous than they were in consumer
services or the entire service sector. Female professionals in the
producer services industries tended to occur in considerably
lower proportion of the total than was the case either in consumer services, in the services sector, or in total employment.
Indeed, only the goods sector had a lower ratio of female professionals. It should, be noted, however, that in the five business and professional services industries alone, the proportion
of female professionals in 1950 was relatively high and in 1960
the level was slightly above that for the entire labor force.

The managerial occupations are more important for males
than for females in almost every industry. In wholesale trade,
the male proportion in managerial positions is considerably
higher than the female. In advertising, almost one-third of the
males are classified as managerial, but almost ten percent of

Table 13a

PERCENTAGE DISTRIBUTION BY OCCUPATION OF MALES EMPLOYED IN SELECTED PRODUCER SERVICES, 1950 AND 1960

	Professional	Managerial	Clerical	Sales	Craftsmen	Operatives	Service Excluding Household	Laborers	All Other	Total
Transportation										
1950	2.0	8.2	12.0	0.3	19.0	38.7	4.0	15.4	0.4	100.0
1960	2.5	8.8	12.3	0.7	17.9	42.7	3.0	11.0	1.1	100.0
Wholesale trade										
1950	2.7	24.3	10.8	24.7	7.1	21.1	1.2	7.9	0.2	100.0
1960	3.4	22.5	10.1	27.1	8.1	19.4	0.9	7.0	1.5	100.0
All producer services										
1950	6.5	14.0	11.3	8.9	14.2	29.9	3.3	11.6	0.3	100.0
1960	10.1	14.0	10.9	10.5	13.3	28.8	3.1	8.0	1.3	100.0
All consumer services										
1950	13.5	19.9	9.2	13.4	13.6	10.2	15.0	4.3	0.9	100.0
1960	16.4	17.6	9.8	12.4	13.6	9.3	14.7	4.6	1.6	100.0
All services										
1950	11.6	18.3	9.8	12.2	13.8	15.5	11.8	6.3	0.7	100.0
1960	14.8	16.7	10.1	11.9	13.5	14.4	11.7	5.5	1.4	100.0
All goods										
1950	3.9	4.6	3.9	1.9	22.8	24.1	1.3	9.5	28.0	100.0
1960	7.0	5.9	4.6	2.8	26.2	26.2	1.3	8.4	17.6	100.0
All employment										
1950	7.3	10.6	6.5	6.4	18.6	20.0	5.9	8.1	16.5	100.0
1960	10.3	10.6	7.0	6.9	19.5	19.9	6.0	6.9	12.9	100.0

Advertising										
1950	19.8	27.4	9.7	20.7	12.8	7.1	0.8	1.3	0.4	100.0
1960	21.9	32.1	9.1	16.6	10.2	5.9	0.7	1.7	1.8	100.0
Miscellaneous business services										
1950	18.4	17.6	13.5	4.4	17.5	11.3	15.5	1.5	0.3	100.0
1960	22.7	14.3	11.5	5.2	15.6	10.7	16.2	2.2	1.4	100.0
Engineering and architectural										
1950	81.7	4.9	2.9	0.8	4.5	4.0	0.3	0.6	0.3	100.0
1960	81.0	5.2	3.2	0.6	5.3	3.2	0.6	0.4	0.5	100.0
Accounting, book-keeping, and auditing										
1950	88.5	3.6	6.4	0.5	0.3	0.3	0.2	n.a.	0.2	100.0
1960	89.0	2.4	7.2	0.3	0.2	0.1	0.1	n.a.	0.7	100.0
Miscellaneous professional services										
1950	83.4	3.8	2.7	0.5	4.6	2.5	1.8	0.4	0.3	100.0
1960	74.6	4.6	4.1	1.2	7.8	3.1	2.3	0.5	1.8	100.0
All business and professional services										
1950	48.4	13.3	8.7	5.6	10.1	6.5	6.2	0.9	0.3	100.0
1960	47.7	11.8	8.3	4.4	10.3	6.6	8.2	1.4	1.3	100.0

N.a.: not available.
Source: Same as for Table 12.

Table 13b

PERCENTAGE DISTRIBUTION BY OCCUPATION OF FEMALES EMPLOYED IN SELECTED
PRODUCER SERVICES INDUSTRIES, 1950 AND 1960

	Profes-sional	Mana-gerial	Clerical	Sales	Crafts-men	Opera-tives	Service Excluding Household	Laborers	All Other	Total
Transportation										
1950	2.5	3.6	71.4	0.4	1.4	9.1	6.2	4.8	0.6	100.0
1960	2.1	3.4	69.8	0.7	0.7	12.0	8.1	1.9	1.3	100.0
Wholesale trade										
1950	1.7	5.0	64.9	4.1	1.2	20.5	1.0	1.4	0.2	100.0
1960	1.5	5.4	69.2	5.1	1.1	14.0	1.3	0.9	1.5	100.0
All producer services										
1950	6.3	5.0	66.2	2.6	1.4	13.3	2.9	2.0	0.3	100.0
1960	6.4	5.1	68.1	2.9	1.2	9.7	4.3	0.9	1.4	100.0
All consumer services										
1950	17.6	5.7	26.4	12.4	0.7	5.3	18.1	0.3	13.5	100.0
1960	18.2	4.6	28.9	11.2	0.6	3.8	19.7	0.2	12.8	100.0
All services										
1950	16.9	5.6	29.2	11.7	0.8	5.8	17.0	0.4	12.6	100.0
1960	17.4	4.7	31.7	10.6	0.6	4.2	18.6	0.3	11.9	100.0
All goods										
1950	2.1	1.3	23.2	0.7	3.3	53.2	1.0	1.7	13.5	100.0
1960	2.7	1.4	29.2	1.3	3.0	51.3	1.2	1.3	8.6	100.0
All goods and services										
1950	12.4	4.3	27.1	8.4	1.5	19.2	12.2	0.8	14.1	100.0
1960	13.0	3.7	29.7	7.8	1.2	15.4	13.5	0.5	15.2	100.0

Advertising										
1950	11.6	9.5	66.6	5.0	1.7	3.2	1.5	0.3	0.6	100.0
1960	11.3	9.8	67.6	4.8	0.9	3.2	0.9	0.1	1.4	100.0
Miscellaneous business services										
1950	11.2	8.2	66.1	1.0	3.5	3.8	5.7	0.2	0.3	100.0
1960	8.6	6.3	66.5	1.7	2.1	5.0	8.4	0.3	1.1	100.0
Engineering and architectural										
1950	12.9	3.3	81.8	0.2	0.7	0.9	0.2	n.a.	n.a.	100.0
1960	14.4	3.4	77.8	n.a.	0.6	1.2	1.6	n.a.	1.0	100.0
Accounting, book-keeping, and auditing										
1950	23.9	1.4	74.1	0.1	0.1	0.3	n.a.	n.a.	0.1	100.0
1960	19.4	1.7	77.1	0.1	n.a.	0.2	0.4	n.a.	1.1	100.0
Miscellaneous pro-fessional services										
1950	65.1	2.5	25.3	2.5	0.8	1.5	3.8	0.1	0.4	100.0
1960	49.5	4.6	38.1	1.1	0.5	1.6	2.0	0.1	2.5	100.0
All business and pro-fessional services										
1950	20.2	6.4	63.2	1.6	2.1	2.7	3.3	0.2	0.3	100.0
1960	14.5	5.7	66.2	1.7	1.5	3.6	5.3	0.2	1.3	100.0

N.a.: not available.
Source: Same as for Table 12.

the females are also so classified, giving advertising the highest female managerial ratio on Table 13.

It is among the female clerical group that the producer services industries show a uniform pattern. The variation from industry to industry among the male clericals is modest. Male clericals are, however, relatively more important in the producer services than in the goods sector or in the total labor force. But among females, the preponderance of clerical occupations in the producer services is striking. The average for all seven producer services industries shows over two-thirds of all females in clerical occupations, as against a range of 29 to 32 percent in the other large groups—consumer services, the services sector, the goods sector, and the total labor force. Moreover, in almost every case, the percentage of females in clerical positions has risen from 1950 to 1960. If the producer services continue to grow somewhat more rapidly than the consumer services and the same occupational ratios prevail, we may look to the producer services as an active claimant for additional female clerical workers.

In the remaining occupational categories, the number of males in sales positions looms relatively large in advertising and wholesale trade, and is below the average in the other industries; the number of female sales workers is below average in all producer services industries, and, as might be expected, well below the prevailing ratios in consumer services. Among males, craftsmen tend to be less important in all types of service industries than they are in the goods sector of the economy as a whole. Male operatives are relatively unimportant in the five business and professional services industries, but they are a relatively high proportion of the total in transportation and wholesale trade. The percentage of male service workers is lower than average in every category except miscellaneous business services, and laborers are significant only in transportation and wholesale trade.

For the male labor force in producer services, then, several patterns emerge. Transportation has an occupational distribution rather like the goods sector. Wholesale trade has its own pattern, with high proportions of managers, salesmen, and operatives. Among the five business and professional services industries, advertising and miscellaneous business services resemble consumer services, while the remaining three industries have their own distinctive pattern of exceedingly heavy professional staffs. The last point is demonstrated more fully by an examination of the 1960 Census reports on the detailed occupations of males in engineering and architectural services on the one hand, and miscellaneous business services on the other. As might be anticipated, in 1960 the male labor force in engineering and architectural services greatly outnumbered the female: 172,987 to 29,257. Among the males, 81 percent were classed as professional, scientific, and technical personnel. Of the 140,158 men in the latter group, engineers constituted almost two-fifths of the total; civil engineers made up the largest engineering specialty. Draftsmen, architects, surveyors, and designers were next in numerical importance; together, these groups comprised over three-fourths of all male employees.

In miscellaneous business services, the 1960 ratio of males to females was less unbalanced; 400,090 males to 233,703 females. In the professional category, over one-third of the 91,000 males were engineers, designers, or engineering technicians. Other significant professional categories were draftsmen, natural scientists, personnel and labor relations men, public relations men, social scientists, and electrical technicians. In this industry, the craftsman group was important, particularly mechanics and repairmen, painters, foremen, stationery engineers, window decorators, and inspectors. Among the 46,000 male clerical workers, such occupations as agents, collectors, messengers, office machine operators, and stock clerks and storekeepers are prominent. Salesmen and auctioneers dominate the sales category. Managers, including self-employed, constitute a sizable group.

From this more detailed account, one can see the variety of occupations and the types of concentration that occur among men in the fastest growing subdivisions of the producer services.

In these producer services areas, the data show that female laborers are of relative importance in both wholesale trade and transportation, while operatives appear to be of more than average significance only in transportation (Table 13). The proportion of women in the "service" occupation was lower than average in every producer service industry except miscellaneous business services, and female craftsmen had lower than average ratios in each of the seven producer services industries.

If we look in detail at the occupational composition of females in two rapidly growing business and professional categories, engineering and architectural services and miscellaneous business services, we see clearly the dominance of the clerical occupations. Of the 29,257 women in engineering and architectural services in 1960, almost 23,000 were clerical workers. Secretaries comprised fully half of the group, and typists, bookkeepers, stenographers, etc., made up the remainder. Two-thirds of the women in miscellaneous business services are clerical workers, receptionists, typists, bookkeepers, telephone operators, stenographers, and office machine operators. General clerical workers far outnumber secretaries. These figures emphasize the diversity of firms in this area of the economy.

It is apparent from this review of the occupational structure of the producer service industries that the faster growing segments utilize highly educated males to a far greater extent than the labor force as a whole, that females with high educational qualifications also have good employment opportunities in these firms, that female clericals are a high proportion of this labor force, and that other white collar and skilled blue collar jobs form a significant part of the total employment picture.

One of our most significant findings concerns the percentage of women in the labor force of the producer services industries. It is considerably lower than the ratio of females in the consumer services industries, and is, in fact, close to the ratio prevailing in the goods sector. As Table 14 indicates, in 1960, 17.5

Table 14

FEMALE WORKERS AS PERCENT OF TOTAL EMPLOYMENT IN
SELECTED PRODUCER SERVICES, 1950 AND 1960

Industry	1950	1960
All producer services	13.6	17.5
All business and professional producer services	29.2	32.6
Advertising	33.4	37.7
Miscellaneous business services	32.3	36.9
Engineering and architectural services	15.4	14.5
Accounting and auditing	25.8	33.2
Miscellaneous professional services	33.4	34.2
Transportation	6.5	8.5
Wholesale trade	19.3	20.2
All consumer services	44.5	48.7
All services	38.5	43.2
All goods	16.8	18.8
All goods and services	28.2	32.7

Source: U.S. Department of Commerce, Bureau of the Census, *Census of Population, 1950* and *1960*.

percent of those employed in the total producer services segment were women, as compared with an 18.8 percent ratio in the goods sector. The average female ratio for all industries was almost 33 percent, the same as the ratio that prevailed in the business and professional producer services.

Focusing on the five business and professional producer services industries, we find that the female ratio in each comes very close to the average for all industries in four cases, but is considerably lower in engineering and architectural services. In transportation, the ratio drops to 8.5 percent, while in wholesale trade the ratio was 20 percent.

A comparison of the 1950 and 1960 proportions of women in various industries indicates a trend toward increasing female employment in all industries but one. We found that this trend is even more marked in the services, both producer and consumer, than in the goods sector. Only one producer services industry, engineering and architectural services, showed an actual decline in the proportion of females between 1950 to 1960.

Most of the men and women on the labor force in producer services industries work in the private sector of the economy, either as employees or as self-employed persons (Table 15). However, a portion of the labor force in the producer services segment works for nonprofit organizations such as universities, research laboratories, trade associations, chambers of commerce, foundations, etc. Since these figures are not available in sufficient detail, the group is included in the private sector. The proportion of government workers (exclusive of those in public administration per se) is much lower than the average in every producer services industry except transportation, communications, and public utilities, where public enterprises exist at all levels of government. But even here, the percent in government employment for all industries runs slightly higher than in transportation.

Among males in the private sector, the relationship between self-employment and employee status is substantially the same for all industries as well as for each of the major components of wholesale trade, of finance, insurance and real estate, and of miscellaneous business services. Only in transportation is the ratio of self-employed much lower than the average, and only in the professional categories, such as legal, engineering, architectural, and other professional services, are the employed and self-employed nearly equal in numbers.

Table 15

EMPLOYEES IN SELECTED SERVICES BY FORM OF
ENTERPRISE AND SEX, 1960

	Total 14 Years and Over	*Percentage Distribution of Males*			
		Private Wage and Salary Workers	*Self Em-ployed*	*Unpaid Family Workers*	*Govern-ment Workers*
Transportation, commerce, and public utilities	100	84.8	4.8	0.1	10.4
Wholesale trade	100	85.7	14.0	0.1	0.1
Finance, insurance, and real estate	100	81.8	15.3	0.1	2.9
Business services, miscellaneous	100	78.8	19.4	0.1	1.8
Legal, engineering, and miscellaneous professional	100	49.4	47.6	0.1	3.0
All industries	100	73.0	15.7	0.5	10.8
		Percentage Distribution of Females			
Transportation, commerce, and public utilities	100	93.4	1.0	0.7	5.0
Wholesale trade	100	94.1	3.2	2.6	0.1
Finance, insurance, and real estate	100	93.7	3.0	1.0	2.3
Business services, miscellaneous	100	87.3	9.8	1.5	1.3
Legal, engineering, and miscellaneous professions	100	85.3	9.4	2.9	2.3
All industries	100	77.7	5.0	2.2	15.0

Source: U.S. Department of Commerce, Bureau of the Census, *Census of Population, 1960.*

The proportion of females who are self-employed tends to
run lower than the ratio for males in every industry; however,
self-employed females are relatively more important in miscellaneous business services and the professional industries than
they are in the total for all industries. Unpaid family workers

are relatively more important among females than males, and in two producer services industries, wholesale trade and the professional fields, the proportion of female unpaid family workers runs slightly higher than the overall average.

Other Demographic Characteristics

To round out the demographic picture, Table 16 provides

Table 16

EMPLOYEES IN SELECTED PRODUCER SERVICES
BY SEX, AGE, AND COLOR, 1960

Industry	Percent Nonwhite Among Males	Percent Nonwhite Among Females	Median Age of All Employed Males	Median Age of All Employed Females
Transportation, communications, and public utilities	9.1	3.8	41.6	34.0
Wholesale trade	7.2	5.1	40.6	38.6
Finance, insurance, and real estate	4.9	3.5	43.2	34.2
Miscellaneous business services	6.3	5.0	39.2	38.1
Legal, engineering, and miscellaneous professional services	2.1	2.3	40.6	37.3
Public administration	10.3	10.9	41.8	41.8
All industries	9.6	12.8	40.6	40.4

Source: Same as for Table 15.

data on the age and race of the personnel in the producer services industries. Producer services which operate chiefly in the private sector tend to employ fewer nonwhites than either industry as a whole or government. In the case of nonwhite males, the employment ratio is conspicuously lower in four producer services industries than in industry as a whole. The employment ratios for nonwhite females are much lower than the average in every producer services category. Victor R.

Fuchs has recently pointed out that for the services sector as a whole, the work force is increasingly being drawn from non-whites.[2] The finding of below average employment of non-whites in producer services is not inconsistent with Fuch's conclusions, since educational requirements are generally higher and also since there has been such heavy employment of non-whites in consumer services.

As far as the age of male workers is concerned, in all of the producer services save one the median age equals or exceeds the figure for all industries. Almost the opposite is true with regard to females. In all of the producer services, the median age is lower than the all industries figure—public administration excepted. On the average, therefore, women in this sector are younger than men by a greater margin than generally obtains throughout industry.

In regard to educational levels the Bureau of Labor Statistics found that in March, 1964 the median years of education for those in the entire professional and technical group was 16.3 years, while managers, officials, proprietors, clericals, and sales workers had a median of 12.5 years.[3] Since all of these groups are overrepresented among the producer services industries and those with only eight to ten years of formal education (operatives, laborers, and farm workers) are underrepresented, it is reasonable to conclude that these industries usually require employees to have a high school education, and often much more.

Median Earnings

Earnings tend to be higher than average in the producer services, largely because of the higher educational levels re-

[2] Victor R. Fuchs, *Productivity Trends in the Goods and Services Sector, 1929–1961: A Preliminary Survey*, p. 29.

[3] U.S. Department of Labor, Bureau of Labor Statistics, Special Labor Force Report No. 53: *Educational Attainment of Workers, March, 1964.*

quired. Median earnings in producer services exceed those for all employees by a considerable margin (Table 17). This holds

Table 17

MEDIAN EARNINGS IN PRODUCER SERVICES,
BY COLOR AND SEX, 1959

	Median Earnings		Nonwhite Median Earnings	
	Male	Female	Male	Female
Manufacturing	$5,135	$2,734	n.a.	n.a.
Transportation, communications, and public utilities	5,285	3,464	n.a.	$3,050
Wholesale trade	5,211	2,895	$2,782	1,704
Finance, insurance, and real estate	5,664	2,931	2,916	2,135
Miscellaneous business services	5,254	2,535	n.a.	n.a.
Legal, engineering, and miscellaneous professional services	7,547	3,125	n.a.	n.a.
Public administration	5,306	3,600	4,506	3,631
All industries	4,621	2,257	2,703	1,219

N.a.: not available.
Source: Same as for Table 15.

true for both sexes, although female earnings are consistently lower than male earnings in the same industries, and female earnings in miscellaneous business services are lower than in manufacturing. For nonwhites of both sexes, median earnings in producer services are also above the average for "all industries." Nonwhite females earn less than nonwhite males in every category.

For reasons which were outlined earlier, services can best be analyzed in terms of a basic consumer-producer dichotomy. The 1960 Census material does, in fact, show that median male earnings in retail trade ($3,871), personal services ($2,975) and entertainment and recreation services ($3,175), are considerably lower than the median earnings in manufacturing ($5,135). But the opposite holds true, as we have indicated, for producer services. Here then, is additional evidence tending to support the view that the producer services group is subject to economic variables which are, to a significant degree, distinct from those affecting consumer services.

Unemployment Rates

To see the employment picture more clearly, we must look at the experience of the business services group with respect to unemployment. This can most readily be done by making use of data prepared by Seymour L. Wolfbein and appearing in his recent book, *Employment and Unemployment in the United States.*[4] Wolfbein showed that for the period covered by his data, 1948–1962, the unemployment rate in the following industries was below the national average in each of the fifteen years: finance, insurance, and real estate; transportation, communication, and public utilities; and public administration. In a general group called "service industries," which includes producer as well as consumer services, the unemployment rate was below the national average in thirteen of the fifteen years. The only group showing a contrary trend, which also includes a sizable proportion of producer services, was wholesale and retail trade, where the rate was above the national average in fourteen of the fifteen years. Here, we suspect that the retail trade group—which possesses a high degree of seasonal as well as cyclical sensitivity, and is not a producer service by definition—is the cause of the poor showing vis-à-vis the aggregate. Overall, as Wolfbein comments, "One will [also] note that the unemployment rate has been mostly above the national average in goods-producing industries and mostly lower than the national average in the service-producing sectors."[5]

Census data on unemployment rates of the experienced labor

[4] Seymour L. Wolfbein, *Employment and Unemployment in the United States,* Table 14-6, p. 306.
[5] *Ibid.,* p. 307.

force for 1950 and 1960 tend to confirm Wolfbein's conclusions. In both years, the unemployment rates for some broad producer services categories were less than those for all industries, as shown in Table 18.

Table 18

UNEMPLOYMENT RATES IN SELECTED PRODUCER
SERVICES, 1950 AND 1960

	1950	1960
Transportation	3.3	3.9
Wholesale trade	3.0	3.3
Finance, insurance, and real estate	1.7	1.7
Business services	3.2	4.0
Public administration	3.1	3.2
All industries	4.7	4.9

Source: U.S. Department of Commerce, Bureau of the Census, *Census of Population, 1950* and *1960.*

From the foregoing data on aggregate employment and unemployment trends, one is led to conclude that the services area, and specifically the producer services segment, presents a picture of strong and persistent past growth, that it enjoys an enviable unemployment rate record, and that these factors are likely to persist in the foreseeable future, making this an area which is particularly attractive to the present and future members of the labor force.

Chapter VI

REGIONAL AND INDUSTRIAL
EMPLOYMENT PATTERNS IN
PRODUCER SERVICES

Our analysis up to this point has proceeded solely in terms of national totals. However, a deeper understanding of the economy and of the conditions affecting economic growth and change can be gained through deaggregating the national totals with the aim of uncovering significant regional patterns. This has particular relevance wherever the investigators have a heightened interest, as in the present instance, in employment, for there are marked differences in the demand for and supply of manpower in the different regions of the country.

The aims of the following analysis will be first to ascertain whether and to what extent employment in producer services is regionally concentrated; next, whether any significant shifts can be found in the locational pattern between 1950 and 1960; and finally, whether certain clues can be identified from an examination of the differential industry patterns which may help to shed light on the process of regional economic growth.

It should be noted that the analyses that can be undertaken are severely limited by the range and depth of the available data. Only through a process of estimating, therefore, will it be possible to derive many of the basic bench-mark data. Implicit in such estimating procedures is the probability of distortions in weights, especially when we are dealing with trend data. Hence, the statistical probes utilized here are significant primarily for the approaches which they open and the gross findings that emerge.

In Chapter II we set out the basic list of industries of which the producer services segment is comprised, together with an estimate of the proportions of the total employed in those industries. The application of this framework, which was derived from national totals, to the separate regions yielded the results shown in Table 19.

As has been noted, there was a slight increase nationally in the ratio of producer services to total employment between 1950 and 1960. Table 19 shows that this ratio increased in each region as well (cols. 7–9). Those regions which had a higher than average ratio in 1950 were Middle Atlantic, East North Central, Mountain, and Pacific. In 1960 three of the four regions again displayed this pattern, but East North Central was replaced by West South Central in this grouping.

In terms of total employment growth between 1950 and 1960 (cols. 1–3), every region showed an increase, but in every case the growth rate of producer services employment exceeded that of total employment (cols. 4–6). For the United States as a whole, the growth of producer services employment was ten percentage points above that of total employment. The individual regions where employment in producer services exceeded total employment by that or by a greater amount were South Atlantic, East South Central, West South Central, West North Central, and Mountain. Of particular significance is the fact that the East South Central region, which had the lowest growth rate in total employment over the decade, 2.9 percent, nevertheless exhibited a 15 percent increase in producer services employment. This statistic takes on added meaning when one considers that the region is undergoing structural changes in the direction away from agriculture. The importance of producer services in this transformation is thereby brought into sharper relief. The West North Central region, second lowest in total employment growth (5.7 percent) also recorded a relatively high increase (14.7 percent) in producer services em-

Table 19

TOTAL EMPLOYMENT AND ESTIMATE OF PRODUCER SERVICES EMPLOYMENT BY REGIONS, 1950 AND 1960

	Total Employment			Estimated Employment in Producer Services			Producer Services as Percent of Total Employment		
	(in thousands)		Percent Change	(in thousands)		Percent Change			Gain
	1950	1960	1950–60	1950	1960	1950–60	1950	1960	1950–60
	(1)	(2)	(3)	(4)	(5)	(6)	(7)	(8)	(9)
New England	3,661	4,138	+ 13.0	485	588	+ 21.2	13.3	14.2	0.9
Middle Atlantic	11,918	13,183	+ 10.7	1,930	2,242	+ 16.1	16.2	17.0	0.8
South Atlantic	7,954	9,510	+ 19.6	1,079	1,482	+ 37.4	13.5	15.7	2.2
East South Central	3,901	4,013	+ 2.9	432	497	+ 15.0	11.1	12.4	1.3
East North Central	11,931	13,403	+ 12.3	1,803	2,109	+ 17.0	15.1	15.7	0.6
West South Central	5,131	5,900	+ 15.0	731	964	+ 31.9	14.2	16.3	2.3
West North Central	5,379	5,683	+ 5.7	658	755	+ 14.7	12.2	13.3	1.1
Mountain	1,794	2,435	+ 35.7	298	457	+ 53.5	16.6	18.8	2.2
Pacific [a]	5,805	8,109	+ 39.7	1,046	1,512	+ 44.6	18.0	18.6	0.6
Total U.S.	57,475	66,374	+ 15.5	8,461	10,605	+ 25.5	14.7	16.0	1.3

[a] Includes Alaska and Hawaii.

Source: Same as for Table 18. Employment in producer services estimated as per Table 2.

ployment. The regions which exceeded the national average in total employment growth over the decade included the South Atlantic, Mountain, and Pacific. These three regions also showed higher than average growth rates in producer services employment. The Mountain and Pacific regions, which exhibited the highest total employment growth rates over the decade of the fifties, also recorded the highest rate of increases in producer services employment.

When the regions are ranked in descending order from highest to lowest employment, we find that in 1950 the following four regions accounted for 65.4 percent of total employment: East North Central, Middle Atlantic, South Atlantic, and Pacific. In 1960 the same four regions accounted for 61.1 percent of total employment—a somewhat lower concentration. However, when ranked by producer services employment, these four regions accounted for 69.2 percent of the total both in 1950 and 1960. That is to say, while the regions in question suffered a slight decline in their share of total employment they retained their share of producer services employment. This factor would appear to be related to the industrial mix of the regions, as well as to some other characteristics of employment in the producer services segment—such as job tenure relationships and similar factors which merit further investigation.

Another way of viewing the changes in employment in producer services relative to changes in total employment is illustrated in Table 20.

On a national basis, roughly one out of every four net new jobs generated over the 1950–1960 decade was in the producer services area (24.1 percent). In six of the nine regions that ratio was exceeded. The highest ratio was found in the East South Central region, where 58.2 percent of the net new jobs (nearly three out of five) between 1950 and 1960 were in the producer services segment. In all probability the government facilities in Oak Ridge, Tennessee and Huntsville, Alabama

Table 20

PRODUCER SERVICES AND NEW EMPLOYMENT,
1950 TO 1960

	Total Net Increase in Employment (in thousands)	Estimated Net Increase in Employment in Producer Services (in thousands)	Increase in Producer Services Employment as Percent of Total Increase
New England	477	103	21.5
Middle Atlantic	1,265	311	24.5
South Atlantic	1,556	403	25.9
East South Central	112	65	58.2
East North Central	1,472	306	20.8
West South Central	769	233	30.3
West North Central	304	97	31.8
Mountain	640	159	24.9
Pacific	2,304	467	20.3
Total U.S.	8,899	2,144	24.1

Source: Same as for Table 18.

were of significance here. The lowest ratio was found in the Pacific region, where only one in every five net new jobs was in producer services—a function probably of the fact that the employment increases there during this period were in the defense oriented, but basically private manufacturing, sectors.

Additional insight into locational factors in producer services employment is provided by the data in the Table 21. From this table we may observe the degree of concentration of producer services relative to each region's total employment in both 1950 and 1960. Coefficients above and below 100 (last two columns) indicate the extent to which employment in producer services was in excess of or below the national average. As of 1960, the regions with the greatest concentration of producer services were the Middle Atlantic with 21.1 percent of total producer services employment, the East North Central with 19.9 percent, the Pacific with 14.2 percent, and the South Atlantic with

Table 21

REGIONAL CONCENTRATION IN PRODUCER SERVICES
EMPLOYMENT

	Percentage Distribution of Total Employment		Percentage Distribution of Producer Services Employment		Convergence index [a]	
	1950	1960	1950	1960	1950	1960
New England	6.4	6.2	5.7	5.5	89.0	88.7
Middle Atlantic	20.7	20.0	22.8	21.1	110.1	105.5
South Atlantic	13.8	14.3	12.7	14.0	92.0	97.9
East South Central	6.8	6.0	5.1	4.7	75.0	78.3
East North Central	20.8	20.2	21.3	19.9	102.4	98.5
West South Central	8.9	8.9	8.7	9.2	97.8	103.4
West North Central	9.4	8.6	7.8	7.1	83.0	82.6
Mountain	3.1	3.7	3.5	4.3	112.9	116.2
Pacific	10.1	12.1	12.4	14.2	122.8	117.3
Total U.S.	100.0	100.0	100.0	100.0		

[a] Convergence index equals region's share of producer services expressed as a percent of region's share of total employment.

Source: Same as for Table 19.

14 percent. A different pattern emerges, however, when we relate the total employment and the producer services distributions. Thus, in 1950, the Pacific region's concentration of producer services employment relative to its share of total employment was the highest in the country. This position was maintained in 1960, although by that year the ratio had dropped slightly. Increases in this ratio over the decade were shown by the Mountain, West South Central, East South Central, and South Atlantic regions. Besides the decrease noted for the Pacific region, decreases were also recorded for the West North Central, Middle Atlantic, and New England regions. The general pattern, then, of producer services relative to total employment as revealed by the shifts in these convergence indexes from 1950 to 1960 is one of a movement toward greater conformity; that is to say, the pattern of employment in pro-

ducer services tended to resemble that of the distribution of total employment.

The general relationships we have been discussing between employment in the producer services sector and aggregate employment on a regional basis must be supplemented by an analysis of the individual industry subgroups which comprise this sector. In Tables 22 and 23 the percent changes and the changed "mix" of producer services employment by component and region are presented.

In the decade of the fifties, the Pacific region showed the greatest percentage gain in total employment—a 39.7 percent increase relative to the 15.5 percent national average. Are there any developments in producer services employment over this period which may help to account for or explain, at least in part, that high growth rate? The data in Table 22 may suggest some answers. In the first place, we may note that the Pacific region differs from every other region in that it recorded the only increase, and a sizable one, in employment in transportation. (This type of infrastructural growth is what one would expect in relatively new and large land areas.)

Second, whereas there was a 25.5 percent increase in producer services employment nationally (Table 19), there was a greater increase than that in nine of the eleven subgroups in this region. Third, the percentage increase in producer services employment, 44.6 percent, was the second highest of the nine regions. By way of contrast, the East South Central region had the lowest increase in total employment (2.9 percent) and it fell below the national average increase in producer services employment in five of the eleven subgroups. In general, therefore, it appears from Table 22 that those regions which showed above average total employment growth rates also showed consistently higher percent changes in producer services employment in all or nearly all of the subgroups. Conversely, those regions which showed lower than average total employment

Table 22
PERCENT CHANGES IN EMPLOYMENT IN SELECTED PRODUCER SERVICES BY REGIONS, 1950 AND 1960

	New England	Middle Atlantic	South Atlantic	East South Central	East North Central	West South Central	West North Central	Mountain	Pacific	All U.S.
Transportation	− 17.8	− 10.8	.0	− 13.5	− 11.4	− 0.3	− 15.3	− 3.5	+ 9.2	− 7.2
Communications	+ 12.7	+ 6.4	+ 36.0	+ 22.3	+ 7.0	+ 8.3	+ 10.3	+ 46.4	+ 34.1	+ 16.1
Wholesale trade	+ 5.7	+ 4.7	+ 24.7	+ 15.5	+ 11.2	+ 24.2	− 1.2	+ 34.9	+ 22.6	+ 13.1
Finance, insurance, and real estate	+ 30.9	+ 22.6	+ 68.3	+ 50.4	+ 34.0	+ 52.5	+ 33.8	+ 77.8	+ 57.1	+ 40.2
Advertising	+ 15.8	+ 17.9	+ 51.1	+ 32.5	+ 1.4	+ 31.7	+ 10.0	+ 47.3	+ 30.3	+ 17.6
Miscellaneous business services	+ 144.9	+ 141.0	+ 224.6	+ 147.9	+ 115.2	+ 145.4	+ 90.5	+ 333.3	+ 217.2	+ 157.3
Legal	+ 18.6	+ 11.7	+ 38.3	+ 21.8	+ 14.6	+ 25.8	+ 14.7	+ 49.2	+ 38.2	+ 21.3
Engineering and architectural	+ 141.2	+ 131.6	+ 159.5	+ 135.5	+ 126.0	+ 119.3	+ 113.8	+ 231.0	+ 174.5	+ 137.5
Accounting, auditing, and bookkeeping	+ 42.5	+ 26.0	+ 82.4	+ 71.4	+ 50.0	+ 72.7	+ 61.8	+ 118.2	+ 63.8	+ 52.8
Miscellaneous professional services	+ 61.9	+ 18.3	+ 86.7	+ 53.0	+ 64.4	+ 56.3	+ 45.4	+ 101.2	+ 96.7	+ 54.6
Government	+ 41.2	+ 34.5	+ 47.3	+ 16.6	+ 38.4	+ 15.1	+ 48.4	+ 85.6	+ 57.4	+ 45.1

Source: Same as for Table 19.

increases over the decade also showed below average growth in roughly half of the subgroups.

In Table 23, each subgroup's percentages of regional producer services employment is given for 1950 and 1960. This then constitutes a regional profile of producer services employment and adds still another dimension to the analysis of employment patterns in this segment.

In view of the nature of the estimating procedures, as well as the fact that these data imply constant proportions of producer services employment by subgroup between 1950 and 1960, the following supplementary observations concerning regional developments should be seen as merely suggestive.

In a comparison of the fastest and slowest growing regions, over the decade of the fifties, the Pacific and East South Central respectively, are there any marked differences observable in the producer services employment mix which may have a bearing on the disparate growth rates? From the data in Table 23, as well as from the national profile worked up in Chapter II, it appears that the Pacific region resembled the national pattern of producer services employment distribution in 1950 in that its top four industries were similar in composition to the national pattern, except for the fact that government employment ranked first instead of second. The major changes in the pattern over the decade are interesting. By 1960, government remained in first position but its share had increased significantly, while the shares of wholesale trade and transportation registered significant declines. There was a slight increase in the relative position of finance, insurance, and real estate; but the most marked changes were a more than doubling in the ratios of the miscellaneous business and the engineering and architectual services.

Unlike the Pacific, the East South Central region exhibited a pattern marked by negligible change in the relative share of government employment over the decade. Another item of in-

Table 23

ESTIMATED PERCENTAGE DISTRIBUTION OF PRODUCER SERVICES EMPLOYMENT BY REGION, 1950 AND 1960

	New England	Middle Atlantic	South Atlantic	East South Central	East North Central	West South Central	West North Central	Mountain	Pacific	All U.S.
Transportation										
1950	21.5	26.5	24.7	29.2	26.2	26.5	29.3	29.1	21.1	25.7
1960	14.6	20.3	18.0	22.2	19.8	20.0	21.6	18.3	15.9	19.0
Communications										
1950	4.8	4.6	3.4	3.4	4.0	4.2	4.0	3.9	4.3	4.1
1960	4.5	4.2	3.3	3.8	3.6	3.4	3.8	3.8	4.0	3.8
Wholesale trade										
1950	23.8	24.1	20.1	22.5	33.0	24.7	25.7	20.3	23.3	25.3
1960	20.8	21.7	18.2	22.6	31.4	23.3	22.2	17.8	19.7	22.9
Finance, insurance, and real estate										
1950	14.5	14.3	9.2	8.9	10.0	9.8	9.8	9.0	11.3	11.2
1960	15.1	15.1	11.3	11.6	11.5	11.3	11.4	10.4	12.2	12.5
Advertising										
1950	1.2	2.2	0.6	0.6	1.6	0.7	0.8	0.6	1.1	1.3
1960	1.1	2.2	0.6	0.7	1.4	0.7	0.8	0.6	1.0	1.2
Miscellaneous business services										
1950	3.1	3.7	2.0	2.0	3.0	2.3	2.1	2.2	3.4	2.9
1960	6.3	7.6	4.7	4.3	5.4	4.2	3.5	6.5	7.5	5.9

Legal									
1950	1.7	1.8	1.2	1.2	1.2	1.2	1.1	1.1	1.1	1.3
1960	1.7	1.8	1.3	1.2	1.2	1.2	1.1	1.1	1.1	1.3
Engineering and architectural									
1950	1.2	1.1	0.8	0.7	0.8	0.9	0.6	0.7	0.7	0.9
1960	2.4	2.0	1.4	1.3	1.6	1.5	1.2	1.5	1.5	1.7
Accounting, auditing, and bookkeeping									
1950	1.1	1.4	0.7	0.7	0.9	0.9	0.7	1.0	1.5	1.1
1960	1.3	1.6	1.0	1.0	1.2	1.3	1.0	1.4	1.7	1.3
Miscellaneous professional services									
1950	0.9	0.9	0.4	0.2	0.5	0.3	0.3	0.4	0.9	0.6
1960	1.1	1.0	5.4	0.3	0.7	0.4	0.3	1.1	1.1	0.7
Government									
1950	26.2	19.4	36.9	30.6	18.8	28.5	25.6	31.2	31.2	25.6
1960	30.6	22.5	39.6	31.0	22.2	32.7	33.1	37.7	37.7	29.7
Total producer services									
1950	100.0	100.0	100.0	100.0	100.0	100.0	100.0	100.0	100.0	100.0
1960	100.0	100.0	100.0	100.0	100.0	100.0	100.0	100.0	100.0	100.0

Source: Same as for Table 19.

terest concerns the miscellaneous business services group which, although doubling its share of the total (from 2.0 to 4.3), was still underrepresented in terms of the national pattern (5.9 in 1960) and of the fast growing Pacific region (7.5 in 1960). Moreover, the transportation and wholesale trade groups together accounted for a greater share in the East South Central than in the Pacific region, a fact which may reflect the still greater relative importance of agricultural activities in the former.

These are the main differences one can discern in the producer services employment patterns in two regions at the extremes of the employment growth scale. Further analysis along these lines may provide additional clues with regard to the type of producer services profile which is most likely to be associated with high regional growth rates. The tentative conclusions one might draw for the interregional and intrasegmental data reviewed here are, first, that employment in the producer services segment as a whole accelerates at a greater rate than total employment in regions exhibiting rising growth rates; second, that producer services play an important role in regions undergoing interindustry shifts in the direction away from agriculture; third, that areas which may be said to have been deficient in producer services are overcoming that shortfall; and fourth, that the intrasegmental shifts in the faster growing regions appear to be in the direction away from transportation and wholesale trade and toward the more "knowledge" oriented industries such as the miscellaneous business and engineering and architectual groups.

Differences in Industrial Employment Patterns

The usefulness of gross regional patterns can be enhanced by exploring the interrelationships which exist between the expansion of employment in various industries under the impact of initial demand, and the corresponding expansion which is generated in producer services employment. The basic approach to these questions is provided by an input-output table from which one can determine "what each industry in the economy buys from every other industry," and also "the employment required per dollar of output for each industry." [1,2]

For the present study, our procedure was to extract those industry inputs which, taken together, approach our working definition of the producer services segment. The industries included in this selection are shown in Table 25. Employment in these industries was then totaled and divided by the total employment generated in a specific industry (per billion dollars of final demand), to form what is here termed a producer services employment input ratio. Table 24 presents the results of this computation with the industries ranked in ascending order of such input ratios; Table 25 presents these data for the producer services groups separately.

The data in Table 24 reveal, for example, that of the total employment generated by sales to final demand in the footwear and other leather products industry, 8.6 percent represents employment in producer services. At the upper end of this table, we find that 45.2 percent of total employment generated by sales of the crude petroleum and natural gas industry are in producer services. On the basis of these relationships, we are in a position to make at least a rough estimate of the future trends in employment in producer services if we have some target programs for the growth of the total economy and of its major components. Of course, such estimating assumes that the relationships among the technological coefficients that were found to exist in the past (i.e. 1958 and 1962 for the present tables) will remain substantially unaltered in the future. The shorter

[1] Jack Alterman, "Interindustry Employment Requirements," *Monthly Labor Review,* LXXXVIII (July, 1965), 841 and *passim.*

[2] Goldman, Marimont, and Vaccara, "The Interindustry Structure of the United States," Table 3, p. 26.

Table 24

PRODUCER SERVICES EMPLOYMENT REQUIREMENTS [a]

Rank		Producer Services Employment Input Ratio
1	Footwear and other leather products	8.6
2	Apparel	8.7
3	Machine shop products	10.1
4	Coal mining	10.4
5	Furniture and fixtures other than household	11.2
6	Livestock and livestock products	11.2
7	Household furniture	11.4
8	Wooden containers	11.9
9	Metalworking machinery and equipment	11.9
10	Miscellaneous fabricated textile products	12.0
11	Aircraft and parts	12.1
12	Stampings, screw machine products, and bolts	12.1
13	Stone and clay mining and quarrying	12.5
14	Electric industrial equipment and apparatus	12.6
15	Radio, television, and communications equipment	12.6
16	Electronic components and accessories	12.6
17	Transportation equipment other than aircraft	12.8
18	Scientific and controlling instruments	12.9
19	Special industry machinery and equipment	12.9
20	Agricultural products other than livestock	13.0
21	General industrial machinery and equipment	13.3
22	Electric lighting and wiring equipment	13.3
23	Materials handling machinery and equipment	13.5
24	Engines and turbines	13.6
25	Lumber and wood products, except containers	13.6
26	Broad and narrow fabrics, yarn and thread mills	13.7
27	Miscellaneous electrical machinery, equipment, and supplies	13.7
28	Miscellaneous manufacturing	14.0
29	Construction, mining, and oil field machinery	14.1
30	Office, computing, and accounting machines	14.2
31	Ordnance and accessories	14.2
32	Other fabricated metal products	14.2
33	Leather tanning and industrial leather products	14.4
34	Forestry and fishery products	14.5

Table 24 (cont.)

Rank		Producer Services Employment Input Ratio
35	Heating, plumbing, and structural metal products	14.6
36	Farm machinery and equipment	14.7
37	Glass and glass products	14.9
38	Optical, ophthalmic, and photographic equipment	15.5
39	Service industry machines	15.9
40	Paperboard containers and boxes	16.2
41	Printing and publishing	16.4
42	Rubber and miscellaneous plastic products	16.5
43	Office supplies	16.5
44	Miscellaneous textile goods and floor coverings	16.6
45	Tobacco manufactures	16.7
46	Food and kindred products	16.8
47	Metal containers	17.9
48	Stone and clay products	18.1
49	Nonferrous metal ores mining	18.3
50	Paper and allied products, except containers	18.5
51	Primary nonferrous metals manufacturing	18.6
52	Motor vehicles and equipment	20.0
53	Primary iron and steel manufacturing	20.1
54	Household appliances	20.6
55	Paints and allied products	21.5
56	Plastics and synthetic materials	22.2
57	Chemicals and selected chemical products	24.1
58	Chemical and fertilizer mineral mining	24.5
59	Drugs, cleaning, and toilet preparations	30.8
60	Iron and ferroalloy ores mining	32.9
61	Petroleum refining and related industries	39.2
62	Crude petroleum and natural gas	45.2

a Includes 20 percent of employment in wholesale and retail trade.

Source: Adapted from U.S. Department of Labor, Bureau of Labor Statistics, *Total Employment (Direct and Indirect) per Billion Dollars of Delivery to Final Demand,* 1962.

the period of the forecast, therefore, the more reasonable the hypothesis; the longer the period the less likelihood that the assumption of stability will hold.

Table 25

PRODUCER SERVICES EMPLOYMENT REQUIREMENTS
BY SELECTED PRODUCER SERVICES INDUSTRIES

Rank		Producer Services Employment Ratio
1	Research and development	31.7
2	Business travel, entertainment, and gifts	60.6
3	Agricultural, forestry, and fishery services	65.0
4	Real estate and rental	70.9
5	Business services	72.9
6	Maintenance and repair construction	76.6
7	Automobile repair and services	79.1
8	Electric, gas, water, and sanitary services	81.7
9	Federal government enterprises	82.1
10	Transportation and warehousing	87.6
11	State and local government enterprises	88.4
12	Radio and television broadcasting	89.5
13	Hotels, personal and repair services, except auto	90.7
14	Communications, except radio and television broadcasting	91.5
15	Finance and insurance	92.2
16	Wholesale and retail trade	92.6
17	Medical, educational services, and nonprofit organizations	92.8
18	Amusements	93.6

Source: Same as for Table 24.

Table 25 opens up a different set of relationships. It suggests the extent to which expansion in any one area of producer services seems to be closely associated with expansion in other areas of the field. The explanation probably lies largely in the presence of common expansionary factors such as growth and density of population, or new technological breakthroughs which influence all industries at the same time. Part of the explanation, however, is to be found in the fact that many producer services are so highly specialized that they cannot grow in isolation. They depend in large measure on external services, which means that if they grow they will stimulate the growth of other producer services symbiotically allied to themselves. This is the burden of the following observation by Hoover and Vernon, which reflects conditions in the New York metropolitan region:

The prevailing pattern for central offices in the Region then is to favor a Manhattan location. And their decision largely determines the location of the accountants, lawyers, advertising agencies and similar specialists who contribute to the operations of the office elite. Of course, there are other reasons why advertising agencies, lawyers and other such groups tend to congregate in a compact urban area. Like the suppliers to the garment trade, they are influenced in their locational tendencies not only by the need to be near their market but also by the need to be near the services on which they in turn draw. The illustrations are legion: the advertising agencies' dealings with free-lance artists and lithographers as well as their dealings with publishing firms, radio and television networks; the lawyers' dealings with printers and with one another; the accountants' dealings with the lawyers, and so on. In each of these cases, there is no practicable way of assimilating the outside services into the firm. And in each case, face-to-face contact is an almost indispensable prerequisite of effective communication.[3]

We were careful to stipulate at the outset of this chapter that it was the approach rather than the specific findings that justified our venturing into a search for regional and industrial patterning of employment in producer services. In summary, it would be well to recapitulate what emerged. We were able to find some important differences in the roll of producer services within the economies of the several regions, and further to identify some important decennial changes. We were even able in a few instances to suggest some of the reasons for such differences in spatial distributions as were found to exist at any point in time as well as for changes over time. Further, through the use of input-output analysis, we were able to discern some apparently significant relations between the growth of employ-

[3] Edgar M. Hoover and Raymond Vernon, *Anatomy of a Metropolis*, pp. 99–100.

ment in producer services in relation to the expansion of industries which they serviced. And finally, we found a high degree of mutual interdependence in that the expansion of any one segment of producer services tended to have an expansionary effect on others.

A thorough exploration of these leads would require much better basic data so that we would not have to work from second and third order estimating. It would involve a line of analysis in which the regional and the industrial data would be dealt with simultaneously, so that more insight could be gained into the specific dynamic factors contributing to the expansion of employment. We believe that much more detailed analyses will be required, not only in the field of producer services but for all the other areas of the economy, if we are to move from the position we are now in (where we have control only over aggregates) to the position we would like to be in; that is, where we can appreciate what happens at the specific levels on which the demand for manpower operates and the suppliers are responsive.

Chapter VII

THE ROLE OF PRODUCER SERVICES IN ECONOMIC GROWTH

Having set out the conceptual and empirical framework of the producer services segment, we are now in a position to examine the more general question of the relationship between the economic activities we have collectively termed producer services and the process of economic growth. Our analysis will proceed from several vantage points: by showing the covariation of some aggregate economic variables with producer services; by an investigation of the role of producer services in the operating decisions of the firm; and by reference to policy questions associated with the attempt to stimulate the economic environment.

Aggregate Economic Behavior

The most widely discussed statement of the relationship between the services as a whole (i.e., consumer plus producer) and the stages of economic development was set out a quarter of a century ago by Colin Clark:

Studying economic progress in relation to the economic structure of different countries, we find a very firmly established generalization that a high average level of real income per head is always associated with a high proportion of the working population engaged in tertiary industries. Primary industries are defined as agriculture, forestry and fishing, secondary industries as manufacturing, mining and building; the tertiary industries include commerce, transport services and other economic activities. . . . The reasons for this growth of the relative number of tertiary producers must largely be sought on the demand side. As incomes rise . . . the demand for such services increases, and being non-transportable they must be supplied by workers within the country concerned.[1]

In a later chapter, Clark defines the content of services more specifically to include, "commerce and distribution, transport, public administration, domestic, personal and professional services."[2] The broad similarity of Clark's services concept to that developed in Chapters I and II is clear. However, because we have made a functional distinction between producer and consumer services, it becomes apparent that more than the "demand side" is involved in seeking explanations for growth in the services sector. Clark apparently assumed an increased demand for services on the part of the consumer in accordance with an "Engels' Law" preferential hierarchy of tastes. The analysis of the growth of the producer services segment leads one similarly to examine the demand side, but in this case the demand originates in firms rather than in households. Since there are obvious differences between the demand for services by firms and the demand for services by households, the differentiation between producer and consumer services should help avoid conceptual errors and oversimplifications.

Closer attention to this functional aspect of the productive process by Clark would have averted some later criticisms of his major thesis. P. T. Bauer and B. S. Yamey, for example, flatly contradict Clark's view by stating: "The proportion of all resources in tertiary production will not provide an index of economic progress," for the reasons that "technical possibilities of substitution between productive resources are obviously possible in tertiary production; and clearly the terms on which labor and capital are available are certain to change in a growing economy."[3] Confusion arises here from the critics' equating

---

[1] Colin Clark, *The Conditions of Economic Progress*, p. 7.
[2] *Ibid.*, p. 338.
[3] P. T. Bauer and B. S. Yamey, "Economic Progress and Occupational Distribution," *Economic Journal*, LXI (December, 1951), 749–50.

services output with a relatively low and stable capital-input to labor-input ratio; or, to state it somewhat differently, between the function of the output and the technical coefficients under which the output is produced.

In support of their critique of Clark's thesis, Bauer and Yamey pointed out: "There are familiar examples on a large scale in domestic services, laundry and repair services and restaurant and retailing services where capital equipment is now used instead of labor." [4] Stigler took this argument a step further by maintaining that "if an industry—like power laundries or cleaning and dyeing establishments—has special machinery complicated and extensive enough to be worthy of study, it is almost enough to classify it as a nonservice industry." [5] Our view is that the classification criterion should be the function or type of output, and not the technique of production, for emphasis on the latter would preclude what we consider to be analytically significant ways of describing our industrial structure. From the point of view of microeconomic analysis, that is in analyzing the pricing and output decisions of a firm, it makes no difference if one abstracts from the type of output, but if the focus is on differential rates of growth of industries and of sectors, then the functional approach becomes a *sine qua non*.

In their article Bauer and Yamey assert: "The only feature common to all tertiary production is that the output is nonmaterial. This does not appear to provide a logical category of significance in the analysis of demand or of economic progress." [6] This is a somewhat extreme statement. Most economists would agree, we feel, that the theory of demand, for example, is greatly enriched by the investigations of consumer behavior which led to the formulation of Engels' Law as well as to more modern statements concerning the differential aspects of con-

[4] *Ibid.*, p. 750.
[5] Stigler, *Trends in Employment in the Service Industries*, p. 158.
[6] Bauer and Yamey, p. 752.

sumer demand for goods and services; and that the analysis of the demand for services by business firms can lead analogously to a similar enrichment of theories concerning business demand. We submit, therefore, that the analysis of economic growth would benefit more from an approach which highlights the salient differences among industries than from one in which such distinctions are ignored.

An attempt to provide long-term statistical data illustrating the relative rates of growth of some major economic variables and of producer services is hampered by the fact that no separation of the services sector between its consumer and producer segments has heretofore been made. Data exist on the service category as a whole, and while these provide some indication of the growing importance of the sector, they do not provide the documentation required for our purposes. The analysis of producer and of consumer services necessitates, as we have emphasized, as disparate and precise a set of conceptual tools as does the analysis of consumer and producer goods. Nevertheless, even fragmentary data may suggest the interaction of strategic economic variables with producer services. Aspects of this relationship may be inferred from the data that follow.

(1) Using relatively short-term data, that is to say, for the decade 1950 to 1960, it has been shown (Chapter II) that in terms of both employment and income producer services grew at a greater rate than the economy as a whole—a 15.2 percent increase for total employment and a 21.3 percent increase for producer services employment; and a 71 percent increase in national income and 90.3 percent increase in income generated in producer service activities.

(2) A secular or long-term comparison of aggregate employment and employment in producer services is shown in Table 26.

While the categories in this table are not the same as those in

Table 26
EMPLOYEES ON NONAGRICULTURAL PAYROLLS, 1919 AND 1963

Industry	1919	1963	Percent Increase
Transportation and public utilities	3,711,000	3,914,000	5.5
Wholesale trade	1,684,000 ('39)	3,119,000	85.2
Finance, insurance, and real estate	1,111,000	2,873,000	158.6
Service and miscellaneous	2,263,000	8,230,000	263.7
Manufacturing	10,659,000	17,005,000	59.5
Federal	533,000 ('29)	2,358,000	342.4
State and local	2,532,000 ('29)	6,841,000	170.2
Government total	2,676,000	9,199,000	243.8
All nonagricultural payrolls	27,088,000	56,643,000	109.1

Source: U.S. Department of Labor, Bureau of Labor Statistics, *Employment and Earnings Statistics for the United States, 1909–64*, Bulletin No. 1312-2, p. xiv.

our definitions, the data are useful for showing the differential rates of growth of some types of producer services. Thus, employment in wholesale trade and especially in transportation and public utilities did not grow as fast as aggregate employment over this 45-year period, whereas employment growth in finance, insurance, and real estate and in government exceeded that of the aggregate. The services and miscellaneous group grew at a rate which was more than double that of aggregate employment, although here consumer as well as producer services are combined.

One very tentative conclusion that may be drawn from these data is that those producer services which are more closely related to goods output *per se* grew at the slowest rate, whereas those less directly tied to production, or to put it differently, those having more to do with the dissemination of knowledge, grew fastest. This appears to be consistent with Denison's and others' findings on the important role of knowledge as an independent factor contributing to economic growth.[7]

(3) Economic development, as is well known, does not proceed simply through quantitative increments to plant and equipment, labor force and other resources. There are also important qualitative changes involved. One of these is the changing input mix of the labor force in the expanding firms. Increased output usually requires the creation of additional departments within the firm, necessitates increased communication within and among departments, and also requires greater specialization of personnel. Added to these factors are the increased record-keeping requirements imposed internally by the needs of the firm as well as externally by the greater role of government at all levels. In an advanced economy, there is the additional need for progressive firms to carry on research and development activities to keep abreast of rapidly changing technology. The response to these stimuli may be observed, for example, in a series showing the increase in nonproduction workers within manufacturing firms, as in Table 27.

During the quarter century from 1939 to 1963, a period marked by very rapid economic growth in the U.S., employees in manufacturing rose by some 70 percent; production workers within this group rose by 51 percent, while nonproduction[8]

[7] Edward F. Denison. "The Sources of Economic Growth in the United States and the Alternatives Before Us," Supplementary Paper No. 13, Committee for Economic Development (1962), pp. 230, 232, 268 and 271. See also the references to Fritz Machlup, *The Production and Distribution of Knowledge in the United States,* in Chapter 1 above, notes 23–25.

[8] The term "nonproduction workers" is used here to denote all those employees who are excluded from the term "production and related workers" on the basic reporting form, Monthly Report on Employment, Payroll and Hours (Form BLS, 790c). Specifically, nonproduction workers include those employees engaged in the following activities: "Executive, purchasing, finance, accounting, legal, personnel, cafeterias, medical, professional and technical activities, sales, sales-delivery (e.g., routemen), advertising, credit, collection, and in installation and servicing of products, routine office function, factory supervision (above the working foreman level)." Unfortunately for our purposes, the BLS definition also includes "force account construction employees" on the firms payroll—employees engaged in construction of major additions or alterations to the plant who are utilized as a separate work force. We do not have the latter

Table 27

RATIOS OF NONPRODUCTION WORKERS TO PRODUCTION
WORKERS IN MANUFACTURING,
1939 TO 1963

Year	Total Employees	Production Workers	Nonproduction Workers	Percentage of Nonproduction Workers
1939	10,278	8,318	1,960	19.1
1940	10,985	8,940	2,045	18.6
1941	13,192	11,016	2,176	16.5
1942	15,280	12,996	2,284	14.9
1943	17,602	15,147	2,455	13.9
1944	17,328	14,740	2,588	14.9
1945	15,524	13,009	2,515	16.2
1946	14,703	12,274	2,429	16.5
1947	15,545	12,990	2,555	16.4
1948	15,582	12,910	2,672	17.1
1949	14,441	11,790	2,651	18.4
1950	15,241	12,523	2,718	17.8
1951	16,393	13,368	3,025	18.5
1952	16,632	13,359	3,273	19.7
1953	17,549	14,055	3,494	19.9
1954	16,314	12,817	3,497	21.4
1955	16,882	13,288	3,594	21.3
1956	17,243	13,436	3,807	22.1
1957	17,174	13,189	3,985	23.2
1958	15,945	11,997	3,948	24.8
1959	16,675	12,603	4,072	24.4
1960	16,796	12,586	4,210	25.1
1961	16,326	12,083	4,243	26.0
1962	16,853	12,488	4,365	25.9
1963	17,005	12,558	4,447	26.2

Source: Columns 1 and 2 from U.S. Department of Labor, Bureau of Labor Statistics, *Employment and Earnings Statistics for the United States, 1909–64,* pp. 32–33.

workers increased by 127 percent. Nonproduction workers constituted 19 percent of total manufacturing employment in 1939, but by 1963 they had increased to 26.2 percent.

---

group listed separately, but since we are of the opinion that they constitute a small proportion of the total, our nonproduction figure is not significantly distorted by their inclusion.

It is also interesting to note that even in industries where total employment has decreased, the ratio of nonproduction to total employees has gone up. In mining, for instance, total employment decreased from 955,000 in 1947 to 635,000 in 1953, but nonproduction workers increased both absolutely and relatively; in absolute terms, they rose from 84,000 in 1947 to 136,000 in 1963; and relatively, from 8.8 percent of total employment in the earlier year to 21.4 percent in the latter.[9]

Taken together, therefore, Tables 26 and 27 suggest that the growth of the economy during this period has been accompanied by an even more rapid growth of producer services, both those that are internal to the firm (represented by the nonproduction worker ratio) and those that are external to it, i.e. services that the firm purchases from other firms. Although we have not attempted to establish a cause and effect relationship among these variables, it appears safe to postulate that the growth of producer services is an inevitable concomitant of aggregate economic growth. The variegated patterns in producer services employment in regions exhibiting wide differentials in growth rates, as illustrated by the data presented in the previous chapter, also tend to support this hypothesis.

The Level of the Firm

In Chapter III the major determinants of the demand for producer services on the part of the firm were discussed. The subsequent material emphasizes the role that producer services may play in the firm's growth.

In a seminal article, George J. Stigler pointed out that when one focuses on the actual "functions or processes which constitute the scope of its [the firm's] activity, it becomes evident that a variety of cost functions [with respect to output] exists; some costs increase with output, some decrease and some are

---

[9] U.S. Department of Labor, Bureau of Labor Statistics, *Employment and Earnings Statistics for the United States, 1909–64*, p. 3.

relatively constant." Stigler goes on to say that firms may not be able to contract out some functions that are characterized by increasing returns, since, "At a given time these functions may be too small to support a specialized firm or firms. The sales of the product may be too small to support a specialized merchant; the output of a by-product may be too small to support a specialized fabricator; the demand for market information may be too small to support a trade journal. The firms must then perform these functions for itself." [10] The crux of the matter, however, lies in what follows:

But with the expansion of the industry, the magnitude of the function subject to increasing returns may become sufficient to permit a firm to specialize in performing it. The firms will then abandon the process and a new firm will take it over. This new firm will be a monopoly, but it will be confronted by elastic demands: it cannot charge a price for the output higher than the average cost of the process to the firms which are abandoning it. With the continued expansion of the industry the number of firms supplying [the] process will increase so that the new industry becomes competitive and the new industry may, in turn, abandon parts of [the] process to a new set of specialists.[11]

In this quotation Stigler provides a classic description of the growth process—one which commences with functional differentiation within a firm, leading to specialization and subsequent fragmentation, and in turn to maturation and functional differentiation once again. The process is spiral-like rather than cyclical in nature in that new goods and services are created along the way. Other growth paths are, of course, also possible, such as growth through mergers or acquisitions, but these do not, as a rule, result in the proliferation of new firms. In most cases the opposite occurs, that is, many smaller firms become consolidated either physically or via the device of a holding

[10] George J. Stigler, "The Division of Labor Is Limited by the Extent of the Market," *Journal of Political Economy*, LIX (June, 1951), 187.
[11] *Ibid.*, p. 188.

company. Finally, a complete mutant may also develop, that is, a firm selling a good or service which was not provided previously, either internally or externally.

While the ability of an external firm to provide services to other firms at a lower cost than can be provided internally is the primary reason for the growth of such firms, it was pointed out in Chapter III that there are a variety of other forces at work which operate in the same direction. Moreover, in Stigler's exposition the new firms result from the expansion of business, which undoubtedly is true, but it is one of the major theses of the present monograph that certain types of producer services firms may themselves play an initiating role in economic expansion.

Dynamic Role

The latter view is supported and highlighted by the arguments advanced in contemporary analyses of the developmental processes in "backward" areas. In the context of that discussion, the terms "infrastructure" and "social overhead capital" are used synonymously to connote investments by government agencies in certain industries or types of economic activity which are presumed to exert a stimulating effect on other industries. As Stephen Enke puts it:

A considerable majority of officials engaged in planning economic development currently subscribe to the view that a large investment now in SOC [social overhead capital] will encourage private investments later. Improved highways may stimulate truck farming, cheaper electric power may encourage light industry, a more frequent and reliable postal service at reduced rates may indirectly subsidize the publication of magazines and the distribution of knowledge. . . . The basic idea is always that by perhaps temporarily overinvesting in SOC capacity, the costs of many indirectly productive activities . . . can be reduced and hence investment in these enterprises encouraged.[12]

[12] Stephen Enke, *Economics for Development*, p. 322.

In underdeveloped areas such services, which require relatively large investments and possess relatively long payback periods, will be undertaken primarily if not exclusively by government agencies; but in the U.S., as has been shown, the private sector supplies the largest share of such services—at least so far as employment is concerned. Apart from the question of their financing, however, is the substantive one of their alleged stimulating effect on other industries. On logical grounds as well as on the basis of the empirical data previously reviewed, we are inclined to an affirmative view. Nor can we see any a priori reasons why these effects cannot equally apply to advanced economies or to underdeveloped areas within them.

When one looks at this matter from the opposite view, that is to say, at the factors that inhibit the growth of firms, the strategic role of certain producer services again emerges. In a recent study of the growth process by the Oxford Economic Research Group it was pointed out: "Given the will to expand, a firm's actual rate of expansion could be limited, it would seem by one or more of four circumstances—shortage of labor or of physical inputs, shortage of finance, the lack of suitable investment opportunities and the lack of sufficient managerial capacity." [13] One of the important conclusions that was derived from a survey of each of these factors was: "There could be no doubt that, for most of the firms dealt with, managerial capacity, in some sense yet to be defined, was the strongest restraint on their rate of growth." [14] This relationship is stated even more forcefully by J. W. McGuire: "Growth of the firm, in the last analysis, is a function of managerial abilities devoted not to the current operations of the enterprise, but to increasing its size." [15] If this be true, then it serves to underscore our

[13] G. B. Richardson, "The Limits to a Firm's Rate of Growth," *Oxford Economic Papers* (New Series), XVI, No. 1 (March, 1964), 9.

[14] *Ibid.*, p. 10.

[15] Joseph W. McGuire, *Factors Affecting the Growth of Manufacturing Firms*, p. 16.

assertion that producer services, whether of routine types (perishable or semidurable) which permit management to specialize on their major areas of responsibility, or consultative services (durable) which provide necessary intelligence to management, are strategic variables which, by serving to increase efficiency, play a major if not dominant role in the firm's growth process.

Policy Implications

The critical role of producer services in the process of economic development has also been commented on, if somewhat negatively, by Stigler:

At present, there is widespread imitation of American production methods abroad and "backward" countries are presumably being supplied with our latest machines and methods. By a now overly familiar argument, we shall often be a seriously inappropriate model for industrialization on a small scale. Our processes will be too specialized to be economical on this basis. The vast network of auxiliary industries which we can take for granted here will not be available in small economies. Their educational institutions will be unable to supply narrowly specialized personnel; they will lack the specialists who can improve raw materials and products. At best, the small economies that imitate us can follow our methods of doing things this year, not our methods of changing things next year, therefore they will be very rigid.[16]

Stigler's contentions here are well taken, and we believe, moreover, that they are applicable to indigenous as well as foreign underdeveloped areas. But his conclusions cut both ways. If the existence of certain "auxiliary industries" (of which producer services constitute a large and important part) is a precondition for an efficiently functioning economic system, then this is a *prima facie* argument for providing subsidies or other incentives to those industries so that they may exist in

16 Stigler, "The Division of Labor Is Limited by the Extent of the Market," p. 193.

the number and variety required to meet the needs of an expanding industrial base. This recognition can lead to a change in traditional policy recommendations concerning types of firms and industries eligible for subsidization—types which have hitherto been largely overlooked. It is certainly novel, for instance, to think in terms of subsidizing management consulting firms, or mailing, maintenance, messenger, or accounting firms; yet without these businesses as Stigler pointed out, modern production techniques would lack the flexibility so necessary for optimum performance.

Too little attention has been paid, in our opinion, to the stimulating role that producer services play in the dynamism of the American economy, in both the private and the public sectors. If the earlier quotation from the Oxford Research Group to the effect that limitations on the management factor are a primary drag on economic growth has validity, then one must recognize not only the different ways in which American concerns have sought to escape from these constraints but also the contribution of new producer services in the process.

In the private sector, one finds that American corporations are willing to recruit very broadly for potential executives as well as for managers with specific qualities and experience. The almost chronic shortage of qualified management consultants, as mentioned in Chapter III, is another manifestation of the critical nature of this type of durable producer service. Shortages exist also in the perishable or semidurable service fields, such as in the routine data processing occupations. The heavy investment of industry internally (i.e., for on-the-job training) and externally in educational programs for its management work force is indicative of the value placed on this type of investment in human capital.

Another way of gaining perspective on the importance of producer services for the continued growth of an advanced economy such as ours is to take note of some of the more important services provided primarily to business by the public sector. Included here are many of the services of the Departments of Agriculture, Commerce, Labor, and Interior as well as those of such independent agencies as the Atomic Energy Commission, the Civil Aeronautics Board, the Export-Import Bank, Federal Land Banks, Federal Reserve Banks, the Federal Aviation Agency, the Federal Communications Commission, the Federal Deposit Insurance Corporation, the Small Business Administration, and many others on the federal level, not to mention state and local agencies. Indeed, our recognition of the extensive commitment by government to this function was one of the reasons we allocated fully one-third of all government personnel to the producer services employment total in Chapter II.

Economists have long recognized the central importance of transportation and banking for the stimulation of economic growth. But recent developments have underscored the importance of a much broader view of the critically important part played by some other producer services. In addition to the aforementioned role of services supportive of managerial functions, attention should be devoted to such fundamental matters as the improvement of the physical environment, more particularly to the assurance of a sufficient supply of clean water; the maintenance of good racial relations since business will not build or expand in areas of social turmoil; and the accessibility of educational, training, and health institutions now so essential for corporations employing a large number of professional and technical personnel. These are but a few illustrations of the strategic role that producer services play in facilitating and stimulating the growth of an economy. (The role of the economist himself in this process should not be overlooked.) There is much that could be learned for both theory and practice from a more thorough analysis of these trends.

Chapter VIII

OVERVIEW AND SUMMARY

Manpower Analysis and Industrial Structure

The foundation on which the foregoing chapters rest is the belief that, to be fully effective, public policies in the manpower field must be rooted in a better understanding of the industrial structure. The dynamics of change in that structure are particularly important, since policy should be responsive to new conditions and to new needs.

One of the most significant of these structural changes, and one which we believe has far-reaching implications for the labor force, is the fact that nearly two-thirds of all American workers are now employed in industries where the final output is not tangible goods but services. Since the demand for labor is derived in large part from the demand for output, a more systematic and analytically useful approach to the study of the economy's demand for services will result in a better understanding of the factors affecting the short- and long-run changes in the demand for labor.

To this end, Chapters I and II explored the problems involved in the definition of services and in the classification of service industries and occupations. That line of inquiry led us to conclude that the general term "services" was too amorphous and ambiguous a concept to be operationally useful for demand analysis. As a corrective, we suggested that services can be distinguished by means of a time dimension analogous to the perishable-durable continuum customarily employed in the analysis of tangible commodities. The full implications of this approach to the concept of services, in terms of structural and cyclical demand changes, remain to be investigated.

Our major line of approach was the differentiation of services output by type of demand, that is to say, whether they are purchased or received for final consumption or as intermediate inputs to the production process. Since producers are not confined to the private sector, attention was paid to the nonprofit and governmental sectors as well. On the basis of this analysis we arrived at the concept of a producer services segment of the services sector of the economy. Chapters III through VII were then devoted to exploring the quantitative and qualitative ramifications of this segment.

Some of the specific findings that emerged from our analysis of these parameters can be summarized.

A sizable proportion of our nation's manpower is employed in industries (in both the profit and nonprofit sectors) which sell or provide services to other firms (also in both sectors). On the basis of the 1960 Census, we found that approximately 8.5 million workers, or about 13 percent of total employment, are employed in what we have termed the producer services segment. Furthermore, during the 1950–1960 decade employment in producer services showed a greater growth rate (21.3 percent) than did total employment (15.2 percent). In fact, one in every four net new jobs between 1950 and 1960 was in an enterprise providing producer services as a final output.

In terms of income, we found that in 1960 about 23 percent of national income was generated in the producer services segment, a larger proportion than its employment share. In contrast, consumer service industries, which accounted for roughly 50 percent of total employment, generated a relatively smaller proportion—only 37 percent—of national income. We see, then, that the average income generated per person employed is significantly higher in the producer services than it is in the consumer services segment.

The demand for external services by a firm or organization is primarily a function of cost considerations, but we also found some important nonpecuniary factors. Some of the conclusions which derived from our case studies of demand determinants are: (1) the existence of developed producer service industries encourages the establishment and growth of firms and organizations which use such services; (2) there is some indication that the demand for external services is less sensitive to declines in economic activity than one might expect; (3) the need for long-range planning is increasingly felt in American industry and is resulting in a greater use of consultative types of producer services; and (4) management often does not know the extent to which it actually depends on and uses external services.

Since most large firms can either perform certain service functions internally or purchase them (contract out), no simple predictions can be adduced from profit or cash-flow positions regarding their demand for external services. However, the economic data which we examined indicates a trend in the direction of a growing absolute and relative importance of producer services in our economy.

An examination of regional employment and industrial patterns revealed that those regions which exhibited high rates of employment growth between 1950 and 1960 were usually those with relatively high concentrations of producer service activities. The data revealed, in addition, that in those regions with high overall growth rates there was a significant tendency for employment in the various producer services groups also to grow quite rapidly. The analysis of industries using relatively large proportions of producer services indicates a close relation between producer services employment and urbanization.

Producer services are seen to play a critical role in economic development both as a catalytic agent and, in some instances, as an initiating factor. This is a result of the fact that producer services (1) reduce the cost of a function formerly performed internally; (2) permit management to specialize and to concentrate its efforts in the primary areas of a firm's activities; and (3) make possible innovations either in organization or in types of output.

Implications for Manpower Policy

Conventional generalizations about the major economic and demographic characteristics of the service industries, involving such variables as employment growth, wages, and educational and skill levels, were found to be at variance with the facts when applied to the producer services segment. This reinforced our belief that producer and consumer services are subject to quite different sets of economic forces. Therefore, policy recommendations, reflecting established doctrine concerning the services sector of our economy, particularly in the manpower field, are likely to be inappropriate when applied to the producer services segment. It would be a mistake, for example, to discourage a region or city from embarking on an effort to expand employment in "services" on the ground that these areas traditionally employ marginal and low wage workers, since, as our study pointed out, there are higher proportions of professionals and higher average earnings in many producer services industries than in the labor force as a whole.

This study also raises a question concerning present policies designed to promote an increased supply of highly trained personnel in the United States via grants, loans, scholarships, and the like, as a means of stimulating economic growth. We have indicated, for instance, that there is a chronic shortage of highly trained personnel in many producer services and that these areas of activity are also vital to the growth of American output and productivity. Therefore, we ought to consider broadening our subsidization policies with the aim of increasing the number of such personnel as those employed in consulting, accounting, and economic and market research.

The producer services segment is composed of heterogeneous industries and groups of industries with wide ranges in educational and skill requirements. Even educationally and otherwise handicapped youths may be employable in the important and growing field of general maintenance. Moreover, with suitable retraining programs, older workers who are displaced from their jobs for one of a variety of reasons may find employment opportunities in producer services industries where, in many cases, job performance is not geared to the demands of assembly line production. Maximum effectiveness of manpower training programs in the services sector will be correctly approached only when cognizance is taken of the basic economic characteristics of its producer and consumer segments.

Implications for General Economic Policy

With few exceptions, general economic policies designed to stimulate secular growth of the economy have been directed to agriculture and to the rest of the goods producing sector. However, due to the many and close linkages that exist between the producer services and goods producing sectors, more attention should be paid to the former. Domestic economic policies such as subsidies, depreciation allowances, or tax credits, designed to stimulate the goods producing sector, may fall far short of their objectives if sufficient producer services are not available to support the effort. Contrariwise, insofar as policies designed to divert resource flows from the services to the goods producing sector (as are currently being pursued in Great Britain)

also cause resources to flow out of the producer services segment (usually not recognized as a distinct entity), they may
produce perverse effects—that is, total output and output per
unit of input may actually decline.

Export and import classifications should be refined to con-
form to the distinction between producer and consumer services, so that we can learn about the role of producer services in
the balance of payments accounts. (For example, the export of
producer services increases each time a domestic consulting
firm undertakes and completes an assignment overseas for a
foreign firm.) This functional breakdown of service exports
and imports should enable us to discern more meaningful patterns in our foreign trade and thus help lay the basis for more
realistic international economic policies.

Directions for Research

With regard to future research, studies should be undertaken
to classify all services on the basis of their degrees of durability. The attempt should be made to develop as much information of this kind for services as we have for goods. Thereafter,
analysis of the supply and demand for services of differing
durabilities can be initiated to determine the extent to which
the durability criterion affects supply and demand relationships.

The next steps in the research sequence would entail trend
and cyclical analyses of firms and industries in the producer
services segment. Important questions to be answered here are
the roles of producer services at different levels of economic
activity and at different rates of overall growth. In particular,
the search for lead-lag relationships between employment and
income changes in producer services and those in consumer
services and in producer and consumer goods industries should
prove fruitful.

Many important questions arise from our regional analysis

and warrant further investigation. For instance, a deeper study of the role of producer services in regions exhibiting fast and slow growth patterns is indicated. Particularly, the locational factors affecting producer services, the extent to which area specialization exists, the interregional flows, and the economic levels and patterns in areas of high or low producer services concentration, all seem to be of significance in the analysis of economic change and growth.

With specific regard to manpower problems, we need to know more about two major aspects: (a) the nature and conditions of employment in firms which supply different types of services—for example, the degree to which the occupational characteristics in firms which supply perishable producer services (telephone answering, routine maintenance) differ from those which supply durable producer services (engineering and consulting); and (b) the nature and conditions of employment in industries which supply services to another firm or a consumer (household). Partial answers to these questions can be found in the foregoing chapters, but more detailed research is required.

General Conclusions

A reassessment of the economic role of services in general and of producer services in particular is long overdue. The conscious or (what is more likely) unconscious bias of economists and of laymen alike in favor of considering tangible output only is an anachronism which must be abandoned if we are to view the modern economic world with objectivity. Increased attention must be devoted to the nature of the output-of-services industries so that more meaningful and accurate measures of total output and of productivity can be developed.

It is axiomatic that good policies depend on good data. Therefore, one of the first steps in a comprehensive manpower program should be the collection and dissemination of data on the basic economic parameters of the service industries. This, in turn, requires a measure of definitional uniformity among collection agencies.

In view of the growing importance of the producer services segment, greater recognition should be accorded it in the regular reporting of the Departments of Labor and Commerce. The data are needed not only for guidance in manpower problems but also in order to increase our knowledge of capital formation, since, as we have indicated, business spending for some types of services are an inseparable and growing part of the investment process.

The principal objective of this study is to open up a series of questions about the important role of producer services in an advanced technological economy. Attention is called particularly to the manpower dimensions of the segment; to the ways in which the growth of producer services influence both the growth of the economy as a whole and its major regions; and in turn, how they are affected by such growth. As in all exploratory efforts, the questions that have been formulated are more explicit than the tentative and partial answers which have been developed. The questions, however, suggest the direction of future work.

BIBLIOGRAPHY

Alterman, Jack. "Interindustry Employment Requirements," *Monthly Labor Review*, LXXXVIII (July, 1965), 841–50.

American Management Association. *Manager Training in Proper Perspective* (brochure)

Association of Consulting Management Engineers. *Growth of Management Consulting Firms in North America, 1910–62* (mimeographed chart).

Barger, Harold. *The Transportation Industries, 1889–1946: A Study of Output, Employment and Productivity*. New York, National Bureau of Economic Research, 1951.

——— *Distribution's Place in the American Economy Since 1863*. New York, National Bureau of Economic Research, 1955.

Bauer, P. T., and B. S. Yamey. "Economic Progress and Occupational Distribution," *Economic Journal*, LXI (December, 1951), 741–55.

Becker, Gary S. "A Theory of the Allocation of Time," *Economic Journal*, LXXV (September, 1965), 493–517.

Berle, A. A., Jr., and Gardiner Means. *The Modern Corporation and Private Property*. New York, Macmillan, 1933.

Cates, David C. "The Service Industries: Classification for Investors," *Commercial and Financial Chronicle*, November 23, 1961, p. 26.

Chandler, Margaret, and Leonard Sayles. *Contracting-out, A Study in Management Decision Making*. New York, Columbia University, Graduate School of Business, 1959.

Clark, Colin, *The Conditions of Economic Progress*. London, Macmillan, 1940.

Dean, Joel. *Managerial Economics*. Englewood Cliffs, N. J., Prentice-Hall, 1951.

Denison, Edward F. *The Sources of Economic Growth in the United States and the Alternatives Before Us*. Supplementary

Paper No. 13, New York, Committee for Economic Development, 1962.

Diamond, Daniel E. "Changing Composition of the Labor Force—The Shift to Services: What Does it Mean?," in U. S. Senate Committee on Labor and Public Welfare, *Selected Readings in Employment and Manpower* (Committee Print, 1964), I, 109.

Enke, Stephen. *Economics for Development.* Englewood Cliffs, N. J., Prentice-Hall, 1963.

Fabricant, Solomon. *The Trend of Government Activity in the United States Since 1900.* New York, National Bureau of Economic Research, 1952.

Fuchs, Victor R. *Productivity Trends in the Goods and Service Sector, 1929–1961: A Preliminary Survey.* New York, National Bureau of Economic Research, March, 1964 (mimeographed).

—— "The Growing Importance of the Service Industries," *The Journal of Business of the University of Chicago,* XXXVIII (October, 1965), 344–73.

Gide, Charles, and Charles Rist. *A History of Economic Doctrines.* 2nd English ed., Boston, Health, 1948.

Goldman, Morris P., Martin L. Marimont, and Beatrice U. Vaccara. "The Interindustry Structure of the United States, A Report on the 1958 Input-Output Study," *Survey of Current Business,* XLIV (November, 1964), 10–29.

Goldsmith, Raymond W. *Financial Intermediaries in the American Economy Since 1900.* New York, National Bureau of Economic Research, 1958.

Guzzardi, Walter, Jr. "Consultants: The Men Who Came to Dinner," *Fortune,* LXXI (February, 1965).

Hollander, Stanley C. *Business Consultants and Clients: a Literature Search on the Marketing Practices and Problems of the Management Research and Advisory Professions.* East Lansing, Bureau of Business and Economic Research, Graduate School of Business Administration, Michigan State University, 1963.

Hoover, Edgar M., and Raymond Vernon. *Anatomy of a Metropolis: the Changing Distribution of People and Jobs within the New York Metropolitan Region.* Garden City, Doubleday, 1962.

Hultgren, Thor. *American Transportation in Prosperity and Depression.* New York, National Bureau of Economic Research, 1948.

Investments in Human Beings." Supplement, *Journal of Political Economy,* LXX, No. 5 (October, 1962, Part 2).

Judd, Robert C. "The Case for Redefining Services," *Journal of Marketing*, XXVIII (January, 1964), 58–59

Kuznets, Simon. *Commodity Flow and Capital Formation*, Vol. I. New York, National Bureau of Economic Research, 1938.

Machlup, Fritz. *The Production and Distribution of Knowledge in the United States*. Princeton, N. J., Princeton University Press, 1962.

Marshall, Alfred. *Principles of Economics*, 9th (variorum) ed. London, Macmillan, 1961.

McGuire, Joseph W. *Factors Affecting the Growth of Manufacturing Firms*. Seattle, Bureau of Business Research, Washington State University, 1963.

National Bureau of Economic Research. *Annual Report for 1955*.

National Industrial Conference Board. "Organization for Legal Work," *Conference Board Business Record*, XVI, No. 10 (October, 1959), p. 463.

———— "Another Look at Leasing," *Conference Board Business Management Record*, November, 1963, p. 47.

———— *Studies in Business Policy*, No. 72 (March, 1955): *Marketing Business and Commercial Research in Industry*.

———— *Studies in Business Policy*, No. 81 (December, 1955): *Company Insurance Administration*.

Nelson, R. W., and Donald Jackson. "Allocation of Benefits from Government Expenditures," in *Studies in Income and Wealth*, Vol. II, pp. 317–27. New York, National Bureau of Economic Research, 1938.

Preston, Lee R., and E. C. Keachie. "Cost Functions and Progress Functions: An Integration," *American Economic Review*, LIV (March, 1964), 100–6.

Richardson, G. B. "The Limits to a Firm's Rate of Growth," *Oxford Economic Papers* (New Series), XVI, No. 1 (March, 1964), pp. 9–23.

Robinson, E. A. G. *The Structure of Competitive Industry*, Vol. VII in Cambridge Economic Handbook Series. London, Nisbet & Co., 1935.

Rusanov, Y. "Allocation of the Soviet Labor Force in Productive and Nonproductive Areas," Soviet Review, II (July, 1961).

Smith, Adam. *The Wealth of Nations*. New York, Modern Library, 1937.

Stigler, George J. *Trends in Output and Employment*. New York, National Bureau of Economic Research, 1947.

———— *Trends in Employment in the Service Industries.* New York, National Bureau of Economic Research, 1956.

———— "The Division of Labor Is Limited by the Extent of the Market," *Journal of Political Economy,* LIX (June, 1951), 185–93.

Studenski, Paul. *The Income of Nations.* New York, New York University Press, 1958.

Taylor, Thayer C. "New Shifts Shaping Industry Markets," *Sales Management,* November, 1963, pp. 45–48.

United Nations. *International Standard Industrial Classification of All Economic Activities.* Lake Success, N. Y., 1959.

U. S. Department of Commerce, Bureau of the Budget, Executive Office of the President. *Standard Industrial Classification Manual.* 1957.

U. S. Department of Commerce, Bureau of the Census. *Census of Business, 1963, Selected Services, United States Summary.* 1965.

———— *Census of Population, 1950.*

———— *Census of Population, 1960.*

———— *Census of Population, 1960: Classified Index of Occupations and Industries, 1960.*

———— *Historical Statistics of the United States, Colonial Times to 1957.* 1960.

———— *Statistical Abstract of the United States.* 1964.

U. S. Department of Commerce, Office of Business Economics. *United States Income and Output.* 1958.

U. S. Department of Labor, Bureau of Labor Statistics. *Employment and Earnings Statistics for the United States, 1909–64.* Bulletin No. 1312–2 (December, 1964).

———— Special Labor Force Report No. 53 (May, 1965): *Educational Attainment of Workers, March, 1964.*

———— *Total Employment (Direct and Indirect) per Billion Dollars of Delivery to Final Demand.* 1962.

U. S. Department of the Treasury, Internal Revenue Service. *Statistics of Income, 1961–62. United States Business Tax Returns.*

Wolfbein, Seymour L. *Employment and Unemployment in the United States: a Study of the American Labor Force.* Chicago, Chicago Science Research Associates, 1964.

Wright, Carroll D. *The History and Growth of the United States Census.* Washington, D. C., Government Printing Office, 1900.

INDEX

Accounting: national, 5, 9, 11; service expenses, 12, 13, 23, 24

Accounting service, 20, 37, 123; employment, 1950 and 1960, 22(*tab*), 26, 29(*tab*); organization types and receipts, 1961–1962, 49(*tab*), 50, 51(*tab*), 54, 55; occupational analysis, 72, 73, 75(*tab*), 76, 77, 79(*tab*), 81(*tab*), 85(*tab*); regional employment patterns in, 100(*tab*), 103 (*tab*)

ACME, *see* Association of Consulting Management Engineers

Administrative producer services, 36–37

Advertising: employment, 1950 and 1960, 22(*tab*), 29(*tab*); direct mail, 33(*tab*), 37; functional classification, 37; organization types and receipts, 1961–1962, 49(*tab*), 51(*tab*), 54, 55; occupational analysis, 72, 73, 75(*tab*), 76, 77, 79(*tab*), 81(*tab*), 82, 83, 85(*tab*); regional employment patterns in, 100(*tab*), 102 (*tab*)

Age, 88(*tab*), 89

Agriculture, 3, 21, 111, 129; employment rates, *vii*; manufacturing and, 18, 19; East South Central, 94, 104; employment requirements, 108(*tab*)

Airlines, 61

Alabama, 96

Allied Maintenance, 69(*tab*)

Alterman, Jack, cited, 105*n*

American Management Association, 65

Appley, Lawrence A., quoted, 65

Architectural services: employment, 1950 and 1960, 22(*tab*); growth rate, 31; organization types and receipts, 1961–1962, 49(*tab*), 50, 51(*tab*), 55; occupational analysis, 72, 75(*tab*), 79(*tab*), 81(*tab*), 83–84, 85(*tab*), 86; regional employment patterns in, 100(*tab*), 101, 103(*tab*)

Armored car services, 37

Arts, 4–9

Association of Consulting Management Engineers, Inc. (ACME), 63–64, 65

Atomic Energy Commission, 124

Atomic waste disposal, 60

Auctioneers, 33(*tab*), 83

Auditing, *see* Accounting

Automobile services, 108(*tab*)

Banking, 20, 37, 124. *See also* Financial services

Barger, Harold, *vii*; cited, 31

Bauer, P. T., quoted, 112, 113

Becker, Gary S., cited, 10, 56

Berle, A. A., Jr., cited, 44

Bookkeeping, *see* Accounting

Building services, 33(*tab*), 37; demand determinants, 41–42; organization types and receipts, 1961–1962, 49 (*tab*), 50, 51(*tab*), 55, 56. *See also* Maintenance services

Burns International Detective Agency, 69(*tab*)

Business services, n.e.c.: employment (1950 and 1960), 22(*tab*), 29(*tab*); national income (1950 and 1960) originating in, 27(*tab*), 28(*tab*), 29; growth rates, 30, 31–34; organization types and receipts, 1961–1962, 49(*tab*), 50, 51(*tab*); occupational analysis, 72, 73, 75(*tab*), 76, 77, 79(*tab*), 81(*tab*), 82, 83–84, 85(*tab*), 86, 87(*tab*), 88(*tab*), 90(*tab*), 91, 92(*tab*); regional em-